WHEN A PERSON DIES

Pastoral Theology in Death Experiences

Robert L. Kinast

CROSSROAD • NEW YORK

To my father who taught me how to die
and to Judith who teaches me how to live

1984
The Crossroad Publishing Company
370 Lexington Avenue, New York, N.Y. 10017

Printed in the United States of America

Library of Congress Cataloging in Publication Data
Kinast, Robert L.
When a person dies
1. Death—Religious aspects—Christianity.
I. Title
BT825.K53 1984 236'.1 84-11431
ISBN 0-8245-0657-X

Contents

Introduction

This is a book of pastoral and theological reflection. It moves from concrete experiences of death through theological reflection on them in order to enter new experiences in a more integrated, faith-filled way. This is a large order. Death continually assaults us with questions that we can never quite answer satisfactorily. And yet we must keep trying to understand and express anew what we believe about death and how we may live that belief.

There are several features of this book that make it different from other valuable works on death. First of all, the focus is on *theological* questions that arise when we experience death. Most of the current literature on death addresses psychological or social-cultural or moral aspects of death. The theological dimension is often underdeveloped or neglected altogether.

Second, in order to make the questions as realistic as possible, each chapter begins with a practical case. These cases are based on my own pastoral experience, but they are intended to be typical of experiences we all have shared. In any event, the cases are analyzed to raise the theological questions that occupy each chapter.

Third, the theological reflection offered in this book is drawn primarily from process-relational thought. This type of thinking is a relatively new development in Christian theology. Its implications for death and immortality have not been drawn out very extensively; so this book is an attempt to contribute to the extension of relational theology in that direction. At the same time, process-relational thought is couched in a very technical and complex vocabulary. In order to avoid unnecessary difficulties, I have tried to use a relational framework without referring to technical vocabulary explicitly.

The final feature of this work is to reflect theologically on different experiences of death according to a set structure: (1) an experience is presented using a case format; (2) the dominant theological questions raised by the case are identified; (3) the response of a typical theology of death is presented, and a response drawn from relational thought is presented; (4) practical implications are suggested. This four-part format structures each chapter. There are two concluding chapters. One interprets the death of Jesus according to the view developed in the book; the other summarizes and compares the typical and relational theological responses to the questions.

For whom is this book intended? Primarily for anyone who asks the questions this book asks. In another sense, for anyone interested in the answers process theology can offer. But overall, I have written for believers who do not necessarily have formal theological training. It is my hope that this book could be used and discussed by clergy and laity alike. Indeed, my ultimate hope is that clergy and laity would read and discuss it together.

Finally, I have written this book for myself. Like many others, I faced a death experience unprepared. When my father died, shortly after I was ordained a priest, I discovered that I had many more questions than answers and that some very safe assumptions about the goodness and permanence of life had been shattered. I have been trying to respond honestly and adequately to that experience ever since. Relational theology has helped more than other approaches, and so I have wanted to share what I think I have seen and felt. This is it.

·1·

A Grandmother's Death
The Question of Meaning

Experience

Imagine a young couple returning home after a weekend trip. They have just been to visit the wife's grandmother who is near death. In fact, they debated about coming home because it seemed the grandmother might not live more than a day or two. As the couple enters their house, the phone is ringing. They look at each other, unwilling to verbalize what they both feel the call is about.

The grandmother's death was expected, but that didn't soften the impact on the couple when the news arrived. As the news came through the telephone, the words had a stunning effect, momentarily suspending everything else, paralyzing all movement and reaction and even feeling for a while. The expected had become real. An eerie finality intruded into the flow of this couple's life experience. The news of someone's death usually has that effect.

In this case the impact was a little stronger because this had been a very special grandmother. Her husband died when he was forty-five, and she never remarried. Nor did she talk much about it. She just seemed to accept her widowhood as the condition of her life and went on from there. She didn't seem lonely or unhappy, mostly because she was always busy making everyone else feel good.

Her home was always open and her kitchen always busy. The

major holidays were celebrated in her home; prospective husbands and wives were always introduced to her early; and no one faced a crisis or important decision without getting her advice. She was truly the center of the family, but not in a controlling or domineering way. In fact, everyone in the family wanted her to be just the way she was. And that made her death even more difficult to accept.

Her good humor and generosity were qualities that inspired the younger members of the family and modeled good parenting for everyone. She had a kind of wisdom that came from mulling over her life experience. She never talked much about herself but always about life and values; and when she spoke, it was with authenticity and enlightenment, drawn from a source that others didn't seem to have.

The only real gap that had developed between her and the younger members of the family was religion. Many of her grandchildren, now adults, questioned beliefs and devotions that she accepted and practiced consistently and without hesitation. They understood and even appreciated her piety and traditional way of expressing her beliefs, but that was certainly not where they were. When she would probe a little about what they actually believed, whether they attended church, how they felt about certain examples of moral permissiveness in society, they tried to be politely evasive. And she didn't push them.

Earlier on this day, when the young couple was saying goodbye, the grandmother confided in them that she knew she would die soon. It was as if she felt she would never see them again, and she wanted them to know how she was at this final moment. She spoke openly and comfortably about dying soon. She kidded that she would not go straight to heaven because there were still a few things she had to make up for before she could "get in." But she was confident that she would indeed see God and join the saints and angels.

Her real desire in sharing her feelings with the couple was to let them know that she would be interceding with God for them. She envisioned her role as a continuation of her efforts on earth to be helpful, to make others happy, to be present, to strengthen them in their own life journeys. That would not change now. In fact, she felt she could do more for them because she could act more effectively and directly in heaven. So her death was a benefit for herself and for them. Despite death's obvious separation, she would still be with them and for them.

As the news of her death began to sink in, the couple recalled this last conversation with her. They marveled again at how sure she seemed to be that there was an afterlife, that it was an appealing, active life, and that she would share in it. They acknowledged their own serious doubts about immortality. And if there was an afterlife, they just couldn't picture it in the familiar, almost folksy way the grandmother did, or as having the meaning for others that she anticipated. Her view seemed like a relic from the past, from a time when people didn't know as much scientifically or philosophically and didn't think critically.

And yet, they also acknowledged that her beliefs enabled her not just to face death but almost to welcome it. The apparent end of her good and happy life actually had positive meaning for her instead of being a negative experience. As they quietly thought about their own deaths, the couple wished they could have her outlook. Or better, an outlook that *they* could genuinely affirm and that could give them the same spirit, the same sense of meaning about death that the grandmother evidenced. They felt caught between an older belief they couldn't really accept with integrity and a possible new belief they didn't yet see clearly. And so they were left with the question: What does it mean to die?

Theological Question

The couple's question arises from their experience of the grandmother's death. Her sense of death's meaning confronted them with their own feelings about what it means to die. They are caught between wanting death to have a genuine, positive meaning and not being able to see what that meaning is. Their grandmother's way of expressing her belief in death's meaning doesn't communicate to them. In fact, it puts them off somewhat, but it doesn't cancel out the question.

People are more prone to think about death's meaning when a good person who has lived a full life dies. In such a case there are no unusual circumstances to claim attention, no overpowering emotions to cope with as there are when a person in good health dies suddenly or a physical disaster kills many people unexpectedly. Death seems more natural when a person has lived a long life. There is, of course, a feeling of loss and the accompanying sadness. But when death occurs in what we take to be typical or ordinary circumstances, it is more likely that reflective questions arise. They may come when the news of a death is first received (as with the couple above), or during the wake and funeral, or on an anniversary, or through some other reminder.

Even in its most natural and familiar setting, however, death is questionable to us—death itself, not just this or that peculiar circumstance of death. Why is this so? We know death is inevitable, and yet we are disturbed when it actually occurs. In fact, to accept death honestly is a hard-won accomplishment in our society. Our impulse is to resist it, to deny its imminence, to question it. We *know* death comes, but we don't *understand* it; we don't grasp its meaning, and that bothers us.

From a theological perspective the question what does it mean to die, is really a threefold question of meaning. One level pertains to the person who dies, in this case the grandmother. What does death mean for her? As described above, it means that she passes from this life and goes to heaven, where she expects to see God, be with the saints, and intercede for her loved ones. She also suggested that the transition from this life to the next may include some type of "making up," probably for her failures and sins during life. This cluster of expectations expresses the meaning of death for the grandmother.

A second level concerns those who survive. What meaning does the grandmother's death have, for example, for her granddaughter and her husband? From the grandmother's perspective, again, her death means that she will *continue* to care for them, help them, support and relate to them, but in a new way. Death means she can be even more for them. The couple is not so sure. Death seems to mean the end of a continuing relationship. They have her memory and her influence in their actual experience of her. In that sense she is still with them. But that presence cannot be renewed, developed, added to. It is finished. They may keep her alive in their memory, but they cannot keep her alive. Nonetheless, death poses the question: Is this meaningful for those who live on? If so, in what sense?

A third level of meaning is not usually raised, at least not explicitly. It is the meaning of a person's death for God. That may sound strange, because we don't usually think of events as being meaningful for God. Meaning is usually associated with human experience, an experience in which meaning is sought because it is not already possessed. But we believe that God is perfect and doesn't need to seek anything. God already possesses everything that is.

And yet, it sounds equally strange to say that an event as important to us as our death has no meaning for God, because meaning also implies value, worth, significance. Since we are made in God's image and possess an irremovable dignity from God, our whole life (including our death) shares in that dignity and is some reflection of God's image. That has to mean something to God. But what?

These three levels of meaning are all contained in the question that arises when a person, like the grandmother, dies. A theological reflection on death's meaning could begin with any one of the three. In a specific instance, like talking with the couple, the starting point would be determined by which level is dominant for them. Apart from such a context, the most appropriate place to begin is with death's meaning for God, because a theological response to the other two levels is derived from that perspective. In addition, beginning with God helps to insure that we follow the correct priority.

It is especially difficult to maintain this priority in questions of death because death so directly affects, threatens, confronts us with our own ultimate meaningfulness or lack of it. The real, personal, psychological needs we have in facing death are not to be swept aside, but the *theological* response to those needs is indeed theological, i.e., it is derived from our experience and understanding of God. That is the source of our response.

This does not mean, however, that in actual conversation or perhaps in counseling, a person begins immediately with reference to the meaning of the grandmother's death for God. In the practical order initial attention is undoubtedly given to the grieving or pained survivors and the meaning of death for them. But from a theological perspective, *what* is offered is grounded primarily in the meaning of death for God.

This is not always the case. In fact, much pastoral guidance tends to focus on interpersonal sharing and helping skills, giving scant attention to the potential contribution of theology in the pastoral care of the grieving and bereaved. Part of the reason for this is that the typical theological explanation of death's meaning seems unsatisfactory, inadequate to the actual experience of death, artificial or forced in attempting to articulate a faith response to the question: What does it mean to die?

One of the reasons why a typical theology of death gives this impression is that it does not explore extensively enough the meaning of death for God. As a result, theology does not cultivate sufficiently its own distinctive contribution to the question of death. What it does offer can usually be formulated and communicated more effectively by the helping disciplines of counseling, caring, supporting, etc.

The task for a theology of death, then, is to explain the meaning of death so that God's primacy is both the source and goal of the explanation from which the theological meaning of death for the person and for the survivors is derived.

Theological Reflection

How does theology typically explain death's meaning? If it is true to its own origins, theology begins with the death of Jesus, for Christianity itself arose as an interpretation of and response to the death of Jesus. That interpretation was (and is) that Jesus, who truly died, was raised from death by God. In this event God manifests the ultimate divine power as the power of life and simultaneously gives us a glimpse into the extent of life itself. The death of Jesus is the occasion for revealing the final mystery of God.

Not surprisingly, therefore, the meaning of Jesus' death is wrapped in that same divine mystery. No human attempt, however inspired, to grasp that mystery can ever be more than partial. Consequently, no single interpretation is adequate or desirable. The more attempts that are made, the more diverse the interpretations that are available, the more enriched is our capacity to enter the divine mystery of life. This is why, beginning with the first, inspired interpretations of Jesus' death, Christians have continually pondered and probed and projected the meaning of death.

In the course of Christian history, theology has tended to shift its focus from Jesus' death as the manifestation of God's glory and life to Jesus' death as a guarantee of *our* eventual glory and life. This shift has been subtle, even unconscious, and never at the expense of actually omitting God's glory from the explanation. But the effect has been in a sense to subordinate God to our need for assurance about the ultimate meaning of our lives.

A typical theology of death affirms that death marks the definitive end of this earthly life. At the same time, in light of Jesus' death, death also marks a transition into a new state of life. Thus, in the classic, liturgical expression, life is not taken away but changed, transformed. What appears to be a termination of life with no further meaning is seen to be the culmination of life with the fullness of meaning when placed in the context of God's plan for creation. It is God who makes the transition happen, but it is we who benefit. Since God is already fulfilled, indeed the perfection of life, the fulfilling of human persons through the paradoxical transition of death is the new, dramatic, striking event that captures our attention.

We never tire of contemplating this gracious action of a perfect God *on our behalf*. But it is our very affirmation of God's perfection that conditions us to shift attention from God to us. Because we believe God is perfect, we conclude that God does not really need us to enhance the divine life. It would seem an affront to suggest that our death can add anything to God's glory or perfection, whereas God can add everything to our death and give it final meaning.

When theology shifts its focus in this way, certain assumptions are carried along. We may begin to assume that God, who is perfect and loving, should prevent death from being too painful for us or that God should make clear to us why death sometimes occurs as it does (unexpectedly, prematurely, accidentally). When these and similar assumptions are not met, we may even begin to call God into question. Sometimes those who do become bitter or despondent or closed to any explanations of God's ways.

This is the classic problem of theodicy—how to reconcile a good and loving God with the experience of human suffering. The problem is ultimately beyond our capacity to understand completely or explain satisfactorily. But the problem is made unduly complicated when we assume that God exists for our welfare and fulfillment rather than the other way around. And yet, our understanding of God's perfection inclines us in precisely this direction.

It would seem then that for theology to express the meaning of death for God, it must address our understanding of God's perfection. If God's perfection can be understood in a way that doesn't lead to the subordination of God to our need for fulfillment, then the meaning of death for God *and* the primacy of God can be simultaneously affirmed. From this vantage point the meaning of death for oneself and for others may be appropriately drawn.

What do we mean when we say that God is perfect? This is an important and tricky question to answer. Inevitably our understanding of God's perfection moves out from our own experience and understanding of our imperfection. Because we are imperfect, our understanding of God's perfection is a projection of what we are not. To this extent, our understanding of God's perfection is how we think *we* would be if we were perfect. But projecting from human imperfection is not necessarily the best way to understand divine perfection. In fact, it may even lead us astray.

What if God's perfection were understood not on the basis of our imperfection but on the basis of our actual, although limited, perfection? We know some things; God knows those things fully. We can do some things; God can do those things fully. We have feelings; God has those feelings fully. In other words, what we are partially, God is fully.

In this approach God's perfection is described in relation to actual human perfections. Perfection has to do with what is rather than what is not. And when *we* think of God's perfection, it is a perfection in relation to what we are. What else God is or how else divine perfection may be understood would depend on other relationships (e.g., the relationships among the three persons of the Trinity or the relationship of God to some other possible form of life).

What does it mean for God to be perfect in relation to our human world of experience? It means first of all that God's perfection *is* in relation to our human world of experience. It is *that* perfection of God that we are talking about. And that perfection is not an exception to our world, a free-standing existence outside the structure of our existence. God's perfection in any other sense is not what is being discussed because it is God's perfection in relation *to us* that is at stake. At the same time God's perfection in relation to us does not mean that God is simply part of our world, more or less like any other part of it. God's perfection is always perfect, complete, full. This fullness may be seen in two ways.

When anything happens, God relates to that event fully. God is aware of everything and everyone that makes up the event. God's knowledge is complete, while we are aware of only some of the factors that make up that event. In the case of the grandmother's death, the couple certainly was aware of many of the factors involved in that event. But neither they nor anyone else nor everybody else together could know everything which comprised *that* event. God's knowledge, however, does include everything in that actual event. God's knowledge is perfect because it includes everything that is actually knowable.

The last phrase is important. God knows everything there is to know in an actual event. And apart from actual events, there isn't anything to know. So to speak of God's perfect knowledge is to say that God knows everything that actual events or experience allows one to know. We know some of it; God knows all of it. Viewed in this way, one could say that God's knowledge (and perfection) is limited, is relative to what is really *there* in reality to know. This *is* a limitation but not an imperfection. If perfection means the fullness of what actually is, then that describes how God relates to us and who God is in our experience. If God could be more in relation to our experience but were not more, then God would be not only limited but imperfect, and no longer God.

What has just been described concerning God's knowledge is true for the other attributes we associate with God. God is all-powerful. This means that in relation to any event, God can do everything which that event allows. God's power is perfect or full, but limited. Only God knows what the limits of a given situation are because only God knows every situation fully. With our partial knowledge and incomplete power, we may expect God to do something that in a given situation, God simply can't do because God's power is *in relation to* us and our situations. God is not outside of or unconditioned by those real situations—at least, not the God we refer to when we talk of the God of our experience.

The same explanation applies to the feelings associated with any event, like the grandmother's death. The couple is in touch with certain of the feelings that are actually generated by the experience, but they are not in touch with all of them. Nor do they feel completely the feelings they do have. God, however, does feel all the feelings in a situation and feels them fully because God is perfect. It may seem strange to say this. Feelings have long been disassociated from God because feelings are changing and perfection is taken to be changeless; feelings are temporary and perfection is taken to be permanent; feelings are uncontrollable and disruptive whereas perfection is taken to be controlling and ordered.

The classic notion of perfection is one way to understand perfection. It is based on a projection of what is deficient in human experience. An alternative understanding is that perfection is everything that is given in human experience, an "everything" that only God relates to but also an "everything" that is limited to each event. This is the first way in which God's perfection may be understood. The second way is closely related to it.

God relates fully to each event that happens and, throughout time, to *all* the events that happen. God's complete knowledge, power, feeling is complete for everything that makes up the actual world, for reality as a whole. Thus, God's perfection is both intensive (each event) and extensive (all events together). It is both singular and all-inclusive. Only God is capable of such perfection, and in the actual world, the world relative to us, that is as perfect as can be.

Seen in this way, God's perfection in relation to us is always growing, expanding, new. As events occur, God relates to each of them fully and relates them to one another in God's own perfect way. Because God's perfection is always relative to what is actually happening and because things are always happening, God's perfection is a very dynamic, changing (without loss), expanding, and including reality. At no moment is anything left out or omitted or beyond God's capacity. But at the same time, what will happen tomorrow is not yet actual and so is not at *this* moment included in God's perfection. Thus, God relates perfectly to the grandmother's death because it has already occurred. God cannot relate in the same perfect way to the couple's death because it has not yet occurred. God does not have an imperfect relation to that event; God has no relation to it at all because it is not yet actual. When it occurs, God will relate to it perfectly. This may seem to put God in a passive, merely receptive position regarding the events of human experience. God's active role in these events will be discussed in subsequent chapters.

This view quite clearly takes God's relationship to us very seriously and tries to understand God's perfection within that context. The result is that each actual occurrence becomes the standard for determining what a perfect, full relationship to that occurrence is. Whatever such a perfect relationship in each case consists of, that is what God's perfection is in that event. Thus, perfection is grounded in both concrete and limited experiences. Concreteness refers to the definiteness, the actuality of an event (like the grandmother's death); limitedness refers to everything that this concrete event can mean—which is not absolutely everything, but everything *this* event means.

One shorthand way of saying this is to speak of God as interdependent. The word dependent feels strange, even erroneous, in reference to God because of the customary understanding of God as outside of or above any needs/dependencies. But in another sense, God is dependent on actual experience in order to know not what things could be but what they actually are. God could know all the possible ways the grandmother might die and experience her death, but God could not know the actual experience of *that* death until the grandmother died. Then God's knowledge can be complete, full, perfect.

Interdependence is another way of saying that God is in relation to us as we are. And the way we are is developing, changing, becoming through our concrete actions. God's perfection in relation to us is perfection in relation to our actual experiences, and these are actual only as they occur. Thus, to be in relationship to us is for God to depend on us and our actual experience, which God then relates to perfectly.

With this view of God's perfection in mind, we can return to the initial theological question: What does death mean for God? Like any other event, death is an actual experience that allows God to relate to us anew. God has never related to anyone in quite the way that the grandmother's death allows God to relate, because there is only one grandmother like this who dies her death only once. God never has and never will again know *this* death experience with all that it contains. God's perfection is thus uniquely called forth, exercised, and enlarged by one more experience.

All this is true of any event in God's relation to us. Is there anything special about death? There is. Death is the event that finally determines what each person's life project actually is. In terms of a typical theology of death, it is the end of a person's life journey. But the emphasis is not on *end* so much as on life journey. Out of all the possibilities that confronted the grandmother, right up to her last moments, which ones would become actual? What would her unique experience be? What *all* would be gathered in by her and become finally her life? The answers to those questions are not knowable until they are made actual, and they don't become actual until she has finally determined who she is, i.e., with no possibility of changing anything further. This is death.

Seen in this way, death gives a person's ongoing life, with its openness to many possibilities for new experience, a final actuality. Only then can one's life experience be fully, perfectly known and related to. This is the unique character of death; it closes the becoming process that characterizes our life. Until this happens, God cannot know a person fully because there is more to come that God awaits. But when the becoming ceases, when there is no more to come, then God can relate to the person perfectly. And if we add that it is God's nature to relate perfectly, that *that* is what God desires in relating to us in the first place, then we might also say that death allows God to be fully God for us.

Put another way, death contributes to God's perfection because it offers God another actual life experience to know fully, to relate to fully, to feel fully. Obviously, God relates fully to each event that makes up a person's life, but God can't relate fully to the person as a whole, complete, actual person until the person is whole, complete, actual—and this occurs at death. Then the person is all the person is going to be and God can relate perfectly to this new, actual reality.

This does not mean that dying is more valuable or desirable than living. To live is to be open to new possibilities and so to be able to create a richer, fuller, more complete life experience than has occurred up to this point. The dynamism and potential of bringing new creations into actuality is always a high value. But that process reaches its highest value when it is finally actualized. For a human person who is a continuous series of many events, the final actualization is death. Until then, the meaning of a given person's life cannot be known; but when that final moment comes, it is more valuable to have lived as fully and as much of one's potential as possible. Death is valuable as the final actualization *of life*, not as something in and of itself.

There is another dimension to death's meaning for God. Through death God relates perfectly to the actual, final life of the grandmother. This experience of the grandmother is added to the sum total of God's relationships to everything else. This is not a mere quantitative addition. Rather God's knowledge, God's power, God's feeling is enriched by the unique experience that *is* the grandmother and that becomes part of God through God's perfect knowledge, feeling, relation to this event. Thus, an apparently isolated event that ends a human life actually is connected to everything else through God and begins a new, qualitative addition to God's relationship with everything thereafter.

This larger vision of interdependence helps us see how death is meaningful for the one who dies as well as for those who survive. For the one who dies, death means that the person makes a definite contribution to God. The grandmother, for example, shaped to some degree God's actual relation to the world through the unique and perfect relation God established with her. That relation could be finally and uniquely perfect only when she died. God never has and never will again have with anyone else the relationship God has with the grandmother.

It is indeed staggering to realize that our lifetime of experiences, assembled in our own definite, novel way, constitute a unique moment *for God* in God's relationship to the world. Moreover, it is a contribution that God desires and, in the sense explained above, depends upon. Viewed in this way, the meaning of death for ourselves is derived from, or is the other side of, the meaning of death for God. We have what God wants—an actual existence that God can relate to perfectly. But this will be seen as meaningful for us only if we want, in the first place, what God wants. If our faith is genuinely theocentric, then for us to contribute to God is indeed the preeminent meaning of our lives. But if our belief in God is to enlist God in helping us get or do what we are incapable of by ourselves, then this view probably won't seem meaningful. Death confronts us with that decision.

In a similar way, the meaning of death for those who survive is derived from the meaning of death for God. Every actual event enriches God's relationship to the world and therefore to everyone and everything that makes up the world. On a human level this faintly resembles maturity. The quality of a mature person's relationship with others is certainly of higher value than the quality of an immature person's relationship. But how does a person become mature? What are all the events, experiences, people that have entered into the maturing process to enable a person to become mature in a way that leads to qualitatively richer relationships?

This analogy is not meant to suggest that God matures as we do, but it may point out how every actual experience that God relates to perfectly (*because* it is actual) enables God to bring that experience along with everything else to future relationships. The following chapters will spell out a bit more what this contribution (through God's relationship) to the world is. For now it is sufficient to note that the meaning of a person's death for others is derived from the meaning of a person's death for God. Thus, God remains primary, and the meaning of death for God is that what was once only potential has become actual—final, definite, concrete, real. When this happens, it enables God to relate perfectly to that event (the person's life as a whole). This simultaneously contributes a new experience to God that reenters the world through God's now enriched and enlarged experience of relationship.

Practical Implication

In the scenario of the grandmother's death, the young couple was left with the question: What does death mean? In light of the theological reflection just presented, how could that question be answered and communicated to the couple?

First of all, it would be appropriate to begin with the obvious fact that the grandmother's death is the end of her life. But there is a not so obvious meaning couched in that fact. The meaning is the value that anything definite, concrete, actual has in comparison to that which is potential, unsettled, unfinished. This difference may be grasped more clearly through comparisons with other experiences. For example, any work of art that is unfinished remains a possibility with uncertain value, whereas a completed work is actual with definite value. A good intention that isn't carried through in practice is not as valuable as a good intention enacted.

Parallels like these might help the couple see that there is an inherent meaning in the completion of something once it is begun. This is true for human life as well, and death is that act of completion. But is there any meaning beyond this inherent sense? There is, and it is primarily the meaning death has for God. The grandmother expressed this level of meaning in her own way. The couple seemed willing to consider some type of connection between God and death. Another way of expressing this connection is that everything we experience, and especially the culmination of our lifetime of experiences, is a contribution to God in the sense that it provides new occasions through which God relates to us.

Each occasion enriches God's perfection and expands God's range of relations to us. This view presupposes that God is really related to us and in some way depends on our actual development as the basis for relating. The God who is in relation to us is always in relation to us, not external to or outside of such relations, only occasionally entering in with us. Moreover, this relational God deals with what is real, actual, given. God, however, sees and does and feels more with every actual situation than we do. In fact, God relates fully, perfectly to our actual condition. What the couple is feeling about the grandmother's death, God is feeling and more. What they see its meaning to be, God sees too, and more. What they can do in response to her death, God can do, and more. God is always relating more fully than we can but never more than reality itself permits. That's what it means for God to relate perfectly to us.

That understanding has the potential of helping the couple sense God's presence in and with this experience. God affirms and shares what they feel and more. If they believe that, then their experience, which coincides with God's, might also open up the possibility for them of experiencing even more in this situation than they do now. By attending sensitively and openly and perhaps in their own way prayerfully to all that this situation holds, they can begin to enter the realm of God's experience and find there a fuller meaning than they had found on their own. If so, the process begins with *their* experience (which is also God's) that they are willing to trust might mean more and lead to more than they initially perceive. If it does, it will be because their own limited perfection moved toward God's limited perfection, and in the transition they came closer to the ultimate level of meaning in death or any other event—its meaning for God, who is primary and from whom all else flows.

·2·

A Boy's Accidental Death
The Question of Why

Experience

Picture yourself in a hospital emergency room. A woman is hurrying down the corridor to a waiting area. She is out of breath as she enters the room, sees her friend, and rushes over to her. They are talking nervously when a doctor appears at the door and asks to see the first woman privately. Her friend knows what he will say and wonders how she will take the news that her small son had been accidentally killed that afternoon.

It all happened so quickly. The mother was in the kitchen and the son was playing in the front yard. He never left the yard when he played, and his mother had a clear view of him from the kitchen window. She just had to keep glancing up from her work to be sure he was still there. Then, in just a matter of seconds, she heard a racing automobile and a loud crash. As she looked up, she saw the front end of the car smashed into the retaining wall next to their driveway—right where her son had been playing.

The driver, an elderly man, had suffered a heart attack and lost control of the car. It veered off the road, picking up speed until it hit the wall. The whole event was a series of arbitrary, accidental, uncontrolled moments of chance. When the mother came back to the waiting room, she was deeply shaken, sobbing and confused about what to do or say. Her friend led her to a private place where they could just be together and express freely all the tangled, powerful emotions that were gushing forth. No other response was appropriate at that point.

This accidental, shocking death was a truly shattering experience for the mother, not only because of the circumstances of that day but also because of the circumstances of her past. She had been rather freewheeling, even reckless, after graduating from high school. She couldn't seem to settle into any direction in her life, drifting instead in and out of different cities and relationships. She had had several sexual affairs; so when she discovered she was pregnant, she couldn't even be sure who the father was.

It was at that time that she became friends with the woman who came to the hospital this day. They felt comfortable together, had similar interests, and just liked being together. After a while, her friend asked if she would like to go to church with her. She didn't pressure, just invited. It was obvious that her friend had deep religious beliefs and wanted to share what was important and meaningful to her, but she did it respectfully, sensitive to the other person's freedom and readiness.

They had talked a lot about the pregnancy and the options before the mother. Largely because of these conversations, the mother decided against abortion and also decided to keep the baby herself and be the best parent she could be. It seemed like she was finally seeing a meaningful purpose for herself and might even be able to make up to some degree for the way she had been living the last few years.

After the baby was born, the mother did begin to attend church with her friend. Among the new acquaintances she made was a young man who seemed to like her a lot. Sensing this, she decided to tell him about her past and her son. She realized the risk she was taking in doing so and expected him to withdraw from the relationship politely. Instead, he expressed his admiration at her honesty and courage. He acknowledged with equal honesty that he could not condone sexual intercourse outside of marriage, but he agreed with her decision to keep and raise the child herself.

Their relationship continued to grow, and eventually he asked her to marry him. She could hardly believe how drastically her life had turned around. So many good, positive things had been happening. All along she had been rethinking her feelings about religion and church and God. Everything seemed tied together. Finally, she joined the church just one month before they were married. Their son became the legal child of both of them. Their married life was very happy, with no major problems—until this afternoon.

In a matter of seconds everything had been reversed. There were so many feelings churning inside the mother. Over and over again she asked the question: Why? Why was he playing right in *that* spot? Why did the car veer in *that* direction? Why did the driver have an attack just *then*? And why a young boy with his whole life ahead of him? It all seemed so arbitrary—or so planned. She felt victimized, powerless, angry, hurt, crushed, resistant, weak, punished, angry, guilty, violated, angry, alone, angry, exhausted, angry.

She bounced off so many feelings all at once. Her friend was sensitive enough not to attempt answering her questions or relieving her feelings. She just shared as fully as she could this deeply painful experience and let the mother say or feel whatever she wanted. She also hoped that when the husband arrived, he might be able to reassure her that everything happens for a purpose and that we don't always understand God's ways. She knew her friend and her husband both believed that, but as she listened to the genuine, painful question—why—she wondered if the answer would be really satisfying.

Theological Question

The mother's question—why—is a natural, spontaneous response to a shocking death like her son's. There was no forewarning, no time to prepare or begin to adjust to the implications, as in the case of the grandmother in chapter one or even in the case of a young person who is expected to die prematurely. A shocking, accidental death generates confusion and a mixture of powerful, upsetting emotions. Somehow, we feel, things shouldn't happen this way. Something is wrong, out of control, unfair, arbitrary. And we want an explanation that will make sense, restore some kind of order, put things in perspective, help us to trust in the ultimate goodness and meaning of life. All that is packed into the little, one-word question—why?

The question usually occurs at two levels. One pertains to the particular circumstances of the death: time, place, cause, conditions. The mother asks: Why was he playing *there*? Why did the car come *then*? Why did the driver have an attack? No matter how the details of the accident might be analyzed and assembled, they just cannot result in a satisfying, intelligible explanation. There are so many variables, so many minor changes that could have been made and the whole accident would have been avoided.

Confronted by such an experience, we face again the extremely fragile, almost accidental, quality of life itself. At any given moment a person's life can end. We all know that, and yet we are so quickly shocked when our vulnerability is realized. It is as if what *could* happen never really *will*. Part of the reason why we ordinarily think this way is that we want to get on with life and can't be preoccupied by what *might* go wrong. So for practical purposes, we act as if the possibility of a shocking, accidental death is merely hypothetical or too remote to be concerned with. Another reason why we think this way is that we really do believe there is an ultimate power in control of things and that this power is a loving, caring, creating God who is trustworthy.

This conviction leads to the second level of the question: Why then do shocking, accidental deaths occur? At this level, it is a question of responsibility. Who or what is responsible for things happening as they do? Who is in charge? A shocking death like the one we are discussing calls into question our understanding of God and how God relates to us. Going back to the previous chapter, we recall that a typical theology of death tends to depict God as being at our service, protecting and guiding us to fulfillment. This impression is strengthened by our understanding of God's perfection. God knows all things and can do all things.

With this mindset, a person who experiences a shocking death, like the mother, faces a real crisis of understanding. If God is all-knowing and powerful and loves us, why does God let things like her son's death happen? Why couldn't God have altered just one of those minor variables and avoided the whole tragedy? This is the problem of theodicy again. How do we make sense of a loving, trustworthy God when things like this happen? To answer that question is the task of theology.

Theological Reflection

Theology typically responds to this question by trying to speak clearly about God and honestly about ourselves. In speaking clearly about God, theology wants to dispel false understandings and affirm true understandings. The two most prevalent false understandings are that God doesn't really care and that God punishes us for our wrongs.

It is understandable that someone like the mother who experiences her son's traumatic death would be prompted to feel that God simply doesn't care about her or her son. God is either uninterested or distracted or too centered on divine fulfillment to be concerned with a single, momentary event. People who genuinely believe in God would hardly adopt this attitude in the blunt form just described. And yet, even for believers, the overwhelming impact of a shocking death can generate such *feelings*.

This becomes evident in people's behavior more than in their words. After an event like her son's death, the mother could begin to act in a very passive or neutral way toward church, religion, God. The pattern is not hostility, anger, resistance to God. It is more like indifference, signaling that if God doesn't care about me, I won't care about God. God just drops out of her attention. This is a form of passive-aggressive behavior, "getting at" God by disregarding, devaluing the place of God in her life.

Persons may go through a phase like this in their attempt to arrive at a more integral understanding of God. Of course, a person may remain indifferent, closed to any explanation of God's positive role in her experience. This is obviously more serious than just going through a phase and would call for more careful counseling or sensitive approach. Nonetheless, a person always has the freedom to choose how to relate to God, and no one else, with however much theological or pastoral truth, can negate that freedom.

Even though theology can recognize this as an inaccurate and inappropriate understanding of God, it may be necessary to give the mother the freedom to back off, to distance herself for a while from direct, active engagement with God. There is no need to rush in and try to change her feelings right away. She probably feels that she has been pushed around enough right now and may even see her indifference as a way of reclaiming some power and control. At least, her feelings may tell her, you can withdraw, and that *is* something you can choose.

If the mother were to go through a phase like this, it might very well lead to a second inappropriate understanding of God—that God punishes us for our sins. This is inappropriate even though it has often been cited in Christian tradition and is found even in Scripture. The accurate point in this is that our sins are not indifferent, neutral events. They do have repercussions, on ourselves and on others. The inaccurate point is that God decides when and where and how we are going to pay for our sins. This whole matter will be taken up in more detail in chapters five and six. For now, it is important to realize that theology does not typically see God as punishing us.

And yet it is understandable how we might think so. The mother, for example, had lived a rather uncommitted and sexually permissive life when she was younger. She had a child outside of marriage and undoubtedly hurt others by her decisions and conduct. She might have felt that her present efforts to live a good life were not sufficient, that God required more of her to make up for her past. Only God knows how much harm our sins cause; only God knows what a just and suitable punishment would be. Except that, in cases like this, the presumed punishment seems far worse than any wrong that was done. Besides, why should innocent people (like the son and the father) also suffer? Are past wrongs undone by increasing (or introducing) present suffering? This is hardly the way a loving, just, caring God would act. Something more than punishment must be involved.

That "something more" is the true understanding of God that theology tries to express. But it is hard to do so concretely because we usually don't know what it is that God is up to when a shocking, accidental death occurs. And so, theology typically affirms that we simply don't know God's ways well enough to offer specific answers. We believe in God, but we do not always understand how God works in relation to us. All we can do is reaffirm our trust and hope in God, ask our questions without expecting or requiring an answer, and await the final day when we shall be able to understand more fully. In short, theology encourages us to appropriate the example of Job and, despite our pain and loss, hold fast to God.

This typical emphasis is not without some further suggestion about how God enters into such experiences. Generally theology tries to see how God helps us to grow as persons and as believers through events like a young son's death. It is not as if God sets out to have the boy killed so the mother and father can mature. It is rather that when the accident occurs, God can help us learn from it and grow through it. What God has to do (or not do) with the accident itself is beyond theology's competence to say.

Thus, typical theology tries to put a shocking death experience in the best possible light vis-à-vis God. In doing so, theology does not wish to deny or minimize the anxiety of the questions or the real depth of the pain that is experienced. It is concerned to dispel misinterpretations of God (as an uncaring or punishing deity) and is willing to stand with no clear and finally satisfying explanation on the side of a God who loves us and cares for us and relates to us in ways we do not fully grasp. In this way, a typical theology of death attempts to speak as clearly as it can about God.

At the same time theology wishes to speak honestly about us. This has to do with our own responsibility for the kind of death described in this chapter. When faced with the question of why does death occur like this (or at all for that matter), a typical theology responds by declaring that the origin of death is sin. Death is one of the effects of sin. This has sometimes been interpreted to mean that if there were no sin, we would not have died in the sense of our bodily system disintegrating. Rather we would have simply passed from this state of life to the next, perhaps as naturally and easily as we pass from infancy to childhood or adolesence to adulthood. Most of the time, however, theology intends something else in saying that death is the result of sin.

A typical theology of death asserts that sin is responsible for the anxiety, the fear, the unwillingness to face death. It is not the fact of death but our feeling about death that has changed because of sin. Why is this? Sin refers to a disruption in our relationship with God. We are responsible for that disruption and don't know for sure what it will lead to. Especially we don't know what it will lead to after we die. Will we still be with God? Will we be cut off? Will we live at all?

These are "unnatural" questions, i.e., they are not part of what we would be thinking about if we were living as God intends. We should be looking forward to our growth into divine life, to each transitional phase that brings us closer, more intimately into union with God. Instead, we are uncertain, mistrusting, fearful. We attach too much importance to the here and now because that may be all we're going to get. We start to compare ourselves with others and judge them as more or less worthy than we of a good life. We see others as competitors or threats to whatever happiness we can claim. Our lives become all jumbled, and we push consideration of death and immortality aside, as if by doing so we can avoid facing these negative feelings. All *that* is the result of sin; death in this sense is the result of sin.

A typical theology of death further explains this influence of sin in a twofold way. The first is original sin. The precise meaning of original sin has been continually discussed. At the present time, theologians using an evolutionary explanation of human creation and development refer to original sin as the origin of our sinful history. This means that for as long as memory can recall, our human experience has been influenced by sin. However it all began, whatever actually occurred at the beginning, the result has been a sinful history.

This original and continuing sinfulness has an enduring, social effect. It partly determines the world or environment into which every person is born. The degree of determination will vary from one situation to another. Not everyone is affected in exactly the same way by original sin; a lot depends on the actual environment in which one is born and lives and what offsetting, counteracting forces of goodness and grace are operative. This variety in the effects of original sin is somewhat different from the classic, metaphysical view of original sin.

Nonetheless, the effect of original sin is one of the "givens" that every person must contend with. The sinful given is often imbedded in unjust or dehumanizing social structures, in prejudicial attitudes, in traditions of hostility or conflict or control. From this point of view original sin might more accurately be described as social sin or, in biblical terms, the sin of the world. It is a recognition that the wrong that our ancestors have committed from the beginning continues on and partially shapes the world in which we live today.

But this is not all. In addition to original sin, there is personal sin. Personal sin refers to the wrongs that are generated by one's own deliberate choices here and now. This is the concrete, recurring, existential dimension of sin that goes along with the historical, environmental, generic dimension of original sin. The two feed each other. We are inclined to commit personal sin because we live in a sinful environment, and the sinful environment is reinforced and extended by our personal sin. It is not always clear how to separate these two influences in order to determine personal responsibility and to work against sinful conditioning.

In the present discussion, it is not necessary to separate them. The point is that death in its negative aspect is the result of sin, both original and personal. Ultimately we are responsible for the death that disturbs us. We are the answer to the question—why? Each death, the grandmother's, the boy's, insofar as it confronts us with pain, loss, ambiguity, suffering, etc., is the result of a whole history of human sin. These events are what sin is and feels like and looks like when its full implications are unraveled.

But where is God in all of this? Does God have no responsibility whatsoever? Is God excused from all implication in our negative experience? And what consolation or help or support can theology offer those who suffer?

If we go back to the explanation of God's perfection outlined in chapter one, we may see some further implications that shed a slightly different light on a tragic experience like the son's accidental death. The main point of that explanation was that God's perfection is limited by the actual events to which God relates. Although God experiences each event (and all events together) to the fullest degree possible, this does not mean that God can intervene directly to make any event turn out one way or the other. But neither is God entirely passive, simply waiting until things happen in order to relate to them in a sort of after-the-fact reaction.

What is God's active role in shaping events? God relates to everything fully. In the case of the son's death, God knows everything that makes that event the actual occurrence it turns out to be. God also feels everything that everyone affected by the event feels. God absorbs the event and everything/everyone connected with it as fully as possible, i.e., as fully as *that* actual event allows because that's all the fullness there is.

When this event occurs, it also finalizes all the possible ways that event could have turned out. Until the very end, it could have gone any number of ways. God, of course, knew all the ways it *could* have gone, but not even God knew ahead of time which way it would go until it went that way. That is what it means to say God's knowledge is perfect, *relative to* actual events. God's knowledge was indefinite as long as the event was indefinite. God's knowledge was definite (and perfect) as soon as the event was definite, complete.

In the process, God was not merely standing by, waiting to see what would happen. God never stands by with us because God is always in relation to us. God was actively, fully involved in every moment and every occasion that made up the total event of the accident. What sort of activity is this? In every instant, because God perfectly knows what has just happened, God sees all the possible results that could follow. And because God *is* all-good and desires only the best for us, God sees which of these possible results would be best. If there are, say, ten possible results, God sees them all and sees them in their priority from most beneficial to least beneficial *for us*.

This ordering of possibilities is part of God's perfection. We, too, glimpse the possibilities that any experience generates, but we usually see only some of them and we may not rank them accurately. Still we do exercise a certain degree of perfection in our ability to foresee and value. But what we do partially, God does completely. Now because we can and do envision new possibilities, God uses this capacity of ours to communicate to us God's own perfect vision of those same (and perhaps additional) possibilities.

Thus, God is constantly involved in every moment, relating fully to our actual experience, drawing from it all the next possibilities for us, ranking them and communicating them to us through our own capacity to do the same thing. How we receive what God offers is influenced by two factors: our limitation and our freedom. As limited persons we do not always see everything or the best things. We are often dominated by the impact of the previous experience and tend to repeat *it* rather than scan really new possibilities. We feel pulled in several directions and grow tired and inattentive. And, of course, we are affected by sin. Any or all of these limiting factors may make it difficult for us to perceive our situation as God does, to harmonize our sense of what the next best possibility is with God's perfect knowledge of what it is.

In addition to our limitations, we are free. Perhaps we do coincide with God's vision; we do sense just as God does what is best. That doesn't mean we will enact it. We are free to do something else, to settle for less, to pursue another possibility. And until we act on our freedom, nothing is definite, nothing is actual. God will not overcome our limitations or usurp our freedom because God relates to us as we actually are—and that is something only we can decide. God does everything possible to enable us with our limitations and freedom to reach the fullest possible experience in every event, but God cannot experience *for us*, in our place. What actually happens is what *we* make happen.

Getting back to the accident, it is conceivable that God could see in those few seconds all that could happen. If the driver had a heart attack and could not control the car, *that* was the actual situation. God could see all the possibilities that situation allowed for. There were probably very few that could be influenced by free choice. The car was basically controlled by physical and mechanical forces. It was going where it was going, and God couldn't do any more than the natural situation allowed.

On the other hand, there were more options available with the son and the mother. Supposedly, God could see that it would be best for the boy not to be killed, and undoubtedly God wanted to communicate this possibility to both. But surely the boy was most attuned to the possibilities of continuing to play and the mother was most attuned to the possibilities of continuing her kitchen work (or answering the phone, or taking a break, or planning the evening menu). Neither one would be remotely attuned to the possibility of the boy's being imminently killed. This is what limitation means. It affects everyone, including God. There is only so much God can do in relation to our *actual* condition.

The limitations described above are no one's fault. They are the result of an extensive pattern of events and choices that go together to form this one, single event. That cluster sets the actual limits with which God works. Mingled into the whole are some elements that might be identified as sinful or the result of sin: a possible negligence by the mother in letting her son play outside because an accident like this *could* happen; the heart attack occurring because the man stubbornly refused to get a checkup after experiencing chest pains—or being unable to get health care because he was poor and could not afford it. Whatever the explanation—mere human limitation or sinful results of our freedom—the actual conditions finally determined which of all the possible outcomes of that moment would be realized. Throughout, God was actively engaged, fully relating to what was real and wanting to lead into the next best possibility for all involved.

That same desire continues after the event, of course. God remains just as actively involved, relating completely to this tragic experience and seeing the next best possibility and communicating it. What God sees and how effectively it can be received by the mother will again be conditioned by both human limitation and freedom. God never tires of relating to us in this way because God's impetus is for the fullest mutual experience of relating that actual circumstances allow. As depicted here, God is supremely realistic but also steadily creative. God abides by reality but seeks the most creative possibility that reality provides. God experiences everything that we do more fully than we possibly can, and this applies to good experiences and bad. Out of that fullness God draws new possibilities, *for us* to be sure, but also for God because God is in relation to us and wants that relationship to be as satisfying as reality allows.

In this view, we have a large say in determining what reality allows. Our say comes with our freedom. By choosing to blend our vision with God's, to attend to God's direction of our life experience, we can condition ourselves and our environment to move more easily into the kinds of experiences that God sees are best for us all. What this means positively will be pointed out as we go along in later sections of this book. At this point, it may be appropriate to say just a word about our freedom to choose *not* to blend our vision with God's and so to orient ourselves and our environment in a different way. In other words, to sin.

A thoroughly relational view of God, such as the one presented in chapters one and two, understands God to be fully involved in every experience without controlling or directing or interfering in the actual construction of experience. The actual construction of experience is a matter of human decision. These decisions are not usually fully conscious, carefully reflected upon choices. Most of the time our decisions come from feelings or impulses or habit or pressure or just a sense of what would be good to do. Nonetheless, we are responsible for our decisions. This is an extremely important responsibility because most of what happens is beyond the influence of our free choice and action. For example, there was very little anyone's free choice could have done about the runaway car once it was out of control.

Consequently, the area where our freedom *is* operative and influential is all the more important because it is a peculiar, special area. Within that area a great deal of the real value and experience of human life is located. This is especially true in the realm of relationships with others. It is already an exercise of our freedom whether we pay attention to the exercise of our freedom and what the quality of our relationships/experiences is as a result. In general, this quality moves on two interconnected levels.

One is the level of our own experience. This means how consciously, how openly, how intently, how deliberately we choose what we do. Obviously, we can't be fully present to every single moment of our experience, but we should be generally alert to our situation, its possibilities, and the sheer feeling of freedom that comes with choosing to do what we do—even if it is something we do habitually (like eating dinner or returning a phone call or worshiping on Sunday). The same is true for something that seems insignificant, like grocery shopping or sending a thank-you card or taking a day off. Everything we do has more value if we do it deliberately, if we consciously choose to do *it* rather than any number of other things.

Why does this have more value? For two reasons. First of all, it makes the act more human. Free choice is a rare gift, entrusted almost exclusively in this world to human persons. To act unfreely, i.e., out of mere habit or control or pressure, is to generate a less than fully human experience. A second reason is that by attending to our options and really choosing freely what we decide to do, we are more alert to all the possible options in every situation. Often this is not very significant, but when a special occasion comes along, a crisis, an opportunity to act in a really important and decisive way, we will be more or less ready to actualize the best possibility in that situation *if* we have been exercising our freedom attentively all along.

So one level of free choice pertains to our own experience and the enhanced quality of that experience if we have been freely, consciously, deliberately generating it. The other level, which is connected with this, is the contribution of our experience to others. Because we are all related, what one person experiences spills over into the environment that others share. The impact may seem slight for any given experience, but over a period of time the impact increases. And, of course, there are certain experiences, like the mother's experience of her son's death, that have a large and immediate impact.

The connecting point is that *what* our intrinsic, internal, personal experience of freedom is, *that* is also what feeds into and shapes the larger environment around us. Thus, if the mother chooses to accept this shocking event and reaffirm genuinely her belief and trust in a loving God, that experience, which is initially hers, becomes ours as it is actualized through her words, behavior, feelings, presence, etc.

The unifying factor in all this is God. It is God who relates fully to each of us and to everything that constitutes our experience. Nothing is lost on God, whereas we only pick up partially what others are experiencing, and we often choose selectively what to attend to within that partial range. Through God everything is always preserved and made available to us because God is always in relation to us, to all of us and to everything that constitutes us.

This view has several implications, like our influence on each other, the value of support and intercessory prayer, the public responsibility we have for our most private actions, the interdependence of each other's fulfillment, etc. These will be explored more fully in subsequent chapters. The main point here is that we are responsible for the quality of experience that constitutes our lives. God is constantly present to us, sharing and offering us from our experience new possibilities for new experience. We are more or less in touch with this activity of God on our behalf. The less in touch we are, the more likely we are to choose a course of action that will result in less than the best future that our actual past makes possible. Eventually such choices could result in a real failure or crisis or even tragedy for ourselves or for others.

The worst situation, in one sense, is when our neglect or refusal to identify with God's direction hurts another. We may not see how it hurts another, the outcome may not be immediate or it may not be directly caused by our action. But the connection is there, and the influence is operative and the responsibility is heightened. In a thoroughly relational world, there are no purely private acts and there is no merely intrinsic wrong. At its deepest level, the son's accidental death is an unavoidable reminder that we are all tied together and the wrongs/sins that abide in our world exact their price. If the price seems unfair or arbitrary or excessive, that is a stark declaration of how responsible we are for our freedom.

Practical Implication

When a person like the mother experiences a shocking death, a great many reactions take place. One of these is the mother's feeling toward God, expressed by the dramatic, unanswerable question: Why? The foregoing theological reflection does not really give an answer to the question but does try to understand the question and interpret it more deeply. In trying to communicate both the understanding and the interpretation to the mother, it would be well to focus on her feelings.

This is where God is too. Everything she feels, God feels and more. The best way to convey this, of course, is to feel with her, or to let her feel with, at, toward us. Words aren't as important in this situation as a genuine presence, open to her and willing to receive whatever she needs to express. In *that* response, she may also be able to feel the God who actually is with her and let go of the God who is not actually anywhere (the indifferent or punishing God).

Her question—why—is also in a sense God's question because God is once again forced to deal with the result of a complex, interwoven history of human failure and sin. Why could not more people have been more attentive, more caring, more deliberate, more concerned for others, more free, more responsible and thus prevented the boy's death? Whatever frustration or anger or helplessness she is feeling, God is feeling too. And so it is all right for her to feel it all because it won't match the depth or extent of God's feeling.

At the same time, her why is interpreted by God in terms of seeing what can be brought out of this situation. What new possibility for life, for experience, for free choice, for affirmation does this actual event allow for? It may be harder to help the mother move in this direction. Her emotions are strong and deep; her energy is flat; her desire is low. And it almost sounds as offensive as an outsider saying, in effect, look on the bright side. Once again, words won't work.

Feeling might—a genuine feeling, freely chosen, that God can interpret this event in the best possible way and will offer that interpretation as a possibility for the mother's own experience. It is a possibility that can offset the accumulation of previous decisions that combined to result in this death. The stakes are high, as always. The mother can adhere to her pain and anger and loss, or she can place all that and all those (including herself perhaps) responsibile for it in the flow of God's new movement. She can either keep her son dead or let his death open up a new possibility for experiencing life.

The mother's choice will be significantly influenced by those around her. Their felt interpretation fills her environment. By their way of being with her, they either make it more likely or less likely that she will choose life. We are all ultimately responsible for one another; and God keeps relating to all of us, in every aspect, all the time.

·3·

A Wife's Premature Death

The Question of Immortality

Experience

A thirty-five-year-old man is sitting in front of the fireplace in his home. It is about 10:00 P.M. The only sounds are the muffled sigh of the burning logs and the occasional wail of the wind outside. It had been cold earlier that day when he buried his wife who had died after struggling for three years against cancer. Their children were staying with his mother-in-law for the night. He welcomed the quiet, the stillness, the time alone. Just then the doorbell rang.

The husband had a pretty good idea who would be on the other side when he opened the door. He invited his pastor in and they sat by the fire, sipping coffee and sharing periods of silence together. The husband seemed to be in control of his feelings and wanted to reflect on what his married life, and especially the last three years, had come to mean.

He and his wife had been married for ten years. They met when he was a commercial airline pilot and she was a flight attendant. They found they had a lot in common, including a strong religious background. They created a deep, loving, compatible relationship and felt their marriage had been very blessed, particularly with their children.

About three years ago the wife had gone for a medical examination because she had not been feeling quite right. She seemed lethargic and had lost some weight. A series of tests revealed that she had cancer, and her prognosis was not good. That news was shocking to her. At first, she thought of not telling her husband. She herself didn't want to believe it was true or that it was as serious as the doctors indicated. Probably something could be done upon further testing, or maybe if she went on some special diet or therapy, the cancer would clear up.

But she couldn't hide her concern, and her husband sensed something was wrong. She hedged, not wanting to worry him or perhaps hear herself say it. This made her feel more uncomfortable, as if she were cheating on him, but she just couldn't believe this was happening. She began to think that maybe God could intervene or that she could be a living sign of God's miraculous power. Maybe God wanted to use her; maybe God was asking something very special of her. She didn't usually think of God like this, but other people seemed to be used in this way. She became more and more confused; then she decided one day to go to her pastor.

She did not know him very well, but she had been impressed by him. He seemed sensitive, concerned, and "with it." Comments from other parishioners confirmed her impression. When she first went to him, she really didn't know what she expected. She just hoped that he could help. He did.

They talked initially about her feelings and her reasons for not telling her husband. The pastor described the typical stages people go through when they are faced with an impending and untimely death. She quickly realized that she had been denying the facts or trying to bargain with God to remove them. Under the pastor's skilled lead, she saw for herself that what she needed to do was accept her death. She also acknowledged that she couldn't do that alone. She needed her husband. And the pastor pledged his support as well.

The first several months after she shared the news with her husband were very trying. They both felt awkward and self-conscious. They became overly sensitive to clichés like "over my dead body" or "drop dead" or when someone would say something about their children graduating from school or planning a career. In general, they were interpreting their lives in a very solemn and sad way.

It was a struggle but with their own good will, effort, and prayer, with the help of available resources, and especially the consistent support and presence of the pastor, they began to emerge to a new level of acceptance. They could speak about death openly. They talked with their children about what the future would be like without their mother; they grew in sensitivity and appreciation of one another and life and everyday events; and most of all, they deepened their experience of sharing one life with God.

Near the end of her life, while she was in the hospital, the pastor visited regularly and kept in touch with her husband. They both felt as though the pastor had shared their experience as fully as a third person could, and they knew his presence had kept their faith strong. When she died, her husband and the pastor were both present, just as they were that morning at the funeral liturgy.

Now that the long period of adjusting and waiting was over, the husband and the pastor wanted to be with each other, to put a final, personal closure on their experience. They knew they had been through something together that was very profound, very unique, something that would change both of them as few other experiences could. The husband seemed most in touch with what it was.

He mentioned that since she died, he had a new sense of his wife's presence in his life. It was a very real presence, not just a memory of her or reminders of how she would say and do things. That too was present and painful, because she was no longer here in that way and never would be again. It was the "and never would be again" that clutched at his heart and thickened his throat and brought tears to his eyes.

But along with those deeply human reactions, there was this other feeling of her real presence. It was strange, although peaceful. And it was unexpected, almost like a gift. This experience led him to ask questions: Am I just imagining this or is there really a new kind of presence I share with her? Does she feel the same thing? Does she feel anything? What kind of experience do the dead have? Do we share in it? What really happens to us after we die? And when I die, will I meet her? Will we be united and know each other? The questions went unanswered as both the husband and the pastor sat before this mystery and stared at the fire.

Theological Question

The questions that the husband asked are all part of the general question of immortality or afterlife. The questions arose for him because of a new experience he had of his wife after her death. Even though he had anticipated her death, the actual experience was different. There were some feelings he had not expected at all. And these led him in a new way into an area of his belief that he had always affirmed and accepted without too much exploration—immortality.

Now, however, immortality took on special importance. It was more than another item in the Christian creed or part of a general value system and interpretation of life. Now, immortality had to do with his wife and their relationship. Often we hear and analyze and affirm certain things, especially elements of our faith, and not really feel their significance until an actual experience makes them relevant to us. But in that existential moment, what we have previously heard or understood may not seem very relevant to the experience itself, or we can't recall anything that may be pertinent from what we know. There is a continual interplay between our experience and our previous learning/reflection. Each helps us appropriate the other in a new way and perhaps see things we never saw before. Every actual experience is a new opportunity to affirm our faith and to understand what it means.

In this case, the question of immortality is threefold. First there is the question of fact. Are we immortal? Do we live on after our death? There is no clear proof to decide this question once and for all. Philosophical and theological arguments in favor of immortality are not self-evident. Everything depends on how the available evidence is interpreted, whether the interpretation comes from the nature of the soul or the promise of God or the resurrection of Jesus. Whether immortality is a fact or not is something we must *decide* upon. This is one of the reasons why death is threatening to many of us. We don't know for sure if there is any life for us after death. We may believe it in faith or be convinced of it intellectually, but we don't have absolute certitude. So when a loved one dies, we feel the question, as the husband did: Is my wife really alive and present or is it my imagination?

The second question about immortality, persuming there is an afterlife, is: What is it like? What is the experience of living after death? Are we conscious and if so, are we conscious all the time or intermittently? Are we conscious of ourselves only, of others who have died, of God? Do we feel space, time, size, location? Is our awareness clear and immediate and concrete or is it vague, dreamy, loose? Are there emotions? Do we change? Is it essentially a continuation of this life or is it a radically new, unimaginable experience? The questions are as extensive as our present experience of life because what we really are asking is how similar afterlife is to our present life.

Many people feel they get a glimpse into this experience when they read (or themselves experience) the accounts of near-death experience. These accounts are undoubtedly revealing and intriguing, but since the persons who had the experience did not fully die, it is hard to conclude much from them about the experience *after* death. The accounts are limited to ***beginning*** a transition from this life to an afterlife.

The third question is clearly related to the second. Is the afterlife connected with the present life? Do those who have died continue to relate to those who have not died? And if so, what is this relationship? How extensive is it? And is it reciprocal? In the first chapter, the grandmother expressed her conviction that she would continue to relate to her loved ones after her death. She envisioned a very close connection between this life and the next. In the present chapter, the husband indicates that he feels his wife still relating to him but in a new way. Is the grandmother's expectation correct or only wishful thinking? Is the husband accurate or only imagining?

The aim of theology is to respond to these questions as clearly and accurately as possible. But this is not easy because theology doesn't have much to go on. God has not been very specific about the experience of the afterlife or the connection between that life and this one. Much is left to our speculation, and speculation on the unknown can give rise to some very inaccurate conclusions. Nonetheless, these are important questions, and theology should have something helpful to say about them. It may even have something new to say.

Theological Reflection

Theology's typical response to the threefold question of immortality is drawn from a combination of philosophy (mostly Greek) and theology (mostly biblical). Philosophy is used to argue that at least the soul is immortal. This is because the soul has no parts. It is, in a technical sense, simple, i.e., uncomposed. Hence, it cannot disintegrate or break apart or die. In this sense, the soul is immortal.

In addition, the soul is understood to be spiritual, i.e., it is not confined to the space-time context of matter. Although the soul is united to the body during a person's earthly life, it is capable of transcending that relationship and existing apart from space and time altogether. Indeed, in the Greek conception of things, this was the goal of soul life: to escape the created world of space and time in order to abide in its proper state of contemplative perfection.

This vision of the ultimate destiny of the soul accented its quality as intelligent and self-conscious. It is the soul that sees, understands, intuits, speculates, and contemplates. These are taken as the highest perfections of the soul and are approximated only slightly in this life, but they may be exercised more fully in the next. In such a view, this life, especially in its material, changing, limiting aspects, is seen as negative. There is no loss in death because all the forces that inhibit the soul's development are discarded. Death is a liberating event that allows the soul to achieve its own potential. Much of this negative attitude toward the material world infiltrated Christian theology, but it never entirely supplanted the biblical appreciation of wholeness and unity, as we shall see.

This cluster of soul attributes frames an image of what life after death may be like. It is unending because the soul cannot die. There is nothing in it that can disintegrate or be dismantled. Similarly, afterlife is unchanging. This does not mean inactive or static. It means that there is no shifting from one condition to another, from good to bad, better to worse, perfection to imperfection. Thus, there is no hunger, no illness, no weariness, no aging, no forgetting, no misunderstanding, etc. Within the range of experience proper to the soul, there is only *that* type of experience, but also within this range there is constant freshness, intensification, growth, satisfaction, delight.

The most important characteristic of afterlife derived from this philosophical view of the soul is that it is conscious. The afterlife is a fully aware experience. This means that our self-awareness, our consciousness that we are acting subjects/persons is also true of our afterlife existence. Thus, the deepest sense we have of ourselves as living beings in time is how we perceive ourselves all the time in the afterlife. Of course, it is hard to imagine an afterlife that would have much interest for us if it were not conscious. But from a strictly philosophical point of view, whether we want a conscious afterlife or not, the nature of the soul insures it.

On the whole, this view of the afterlife has not been terribly appealing to most people. It sounds so removed, so distant, so abstract when compared with the human experiences that mean the most to us. Sometimes this view has even led people to deny their best human experiences and to try to act in this life as if they were already in the next life. But apart from such aberrations, this vision of afterlife just seems boring and not very attractive. And that is understandable because this description does not present the whole picture. A typical theology of immortality, drawing upon divine revelation as well as Greek philosophy, does present the whole picture.

There is more to the human person than the soul. This is what God has revealed to us, and theology affirms it by remaining in touch with God's revelation in Scripture. The decisive testimony for Christians, of course, in this regard comes in reference to Jesus and what happened after his death. This central mystery of Christian belief is not easily or totally understood, nor do the Scriptures present a unified, crystal-clear explanation. What they do say, however, is that Jesus truly lives after his death, and it is the same, whole Jesus who lives, although he is now in a radically new relationship both to God and to his friends.

The primary way the Scriptures describe this is through the language and imagery of resurrection, which in turn is based on the experience of waking from sleep or coming to consciousness from an unconscious state. This was not completely adequate to express the first believers' experience of the event, but it seemed to be more adequate than any other language at their disposal. The first believers were limited by their actual condition too. Resurrection certainly implies that there is life after death, just as there is waking after sleep. And resurrection assumes that it is the same, whole person who lives just as it is the same, whole person who awakens.

Resurrection does not express quite so clearly or obviously that the resurrected one is in a radically new relationship with others. In fact, resurrection is more likely to suggest that a person is resuscitated, renewed, restored to the same, even if refreshed, relationship as before. The resurrection of Jesus is something other than this. Of course, what examples or language drawn from our experience in this life *would* be adequate to express an experience none of us has had? The challenge in using resurrection language is to remember that resurrection means a new relationship.

This is where the philosophical notion of immortality connects. Resurrection and immortality are not exactly the same. Immortality defines the nature, the essence of something (like the soul) because of what it already is. It will never die or cease to be. But something could be immortal without being resurrected. Resurrection refers to a particular way of becoming immortal—not by nature but by a special act. The act is special because it is not necessary and because it cannot be performed by the one who is resurrected. Typical theology expresses these two characteristics of resurrection as grace and divine power.

Thus, the resurrection of Jesus means that God graciously raised Jesus from death to immortal life. In doing so, God bestowed on Jesus a new relationship, one we acknowledge by the title Lord. In the resurrection of Jesus, Christians believe, God also revealed the destiny intended for each one of us. Beyond these assertions, a typical theology of immortality can't be much more specific. It can, however, speculate. If we were to speculate further about immortality using the general relational approach of the previous chapters, what else might we say?

In a thoroughly relational view, everything depends on the relations. As long as a person, like the wife, is in relationship (to her husband, to the pastor, to her children, etc.), she is actual or alive. But when she dies, her relationality appears to die with her. She is no longer an active, deciding, feeling, responding agent. This does not mean that her death has no meaning. As described in chapter one, her death has meaning for God, for herself, and for others, but it is the meaning of her life as lived. That is finalized at death. When the conditions that enable her to relate break down and stop functioning, she dies—she ceases to be in active relationship.

In such a view, there is no natural, necessary immortality, as in the classic philosophical view. There is no aspect of the wife's relationality that somehow transcends the structure of her relationships and continues to exist on its own. She *is* what her relationships have been, and apart from them she is no longer. This is another way of saying that death is the end of our earthly journey. We truly cease to become when we die.

If immortality is to be maintained consistently in this approach, it must come from a source other than the person who dies. The survivors cannot bestow immortality. Even if they could keep the wife alive in memory for a while, they themselves are mortal, and eventually the memory would fade as it is passed on. Whatever immortality this kind of action generates, it would eventually cease. What about famous people whose memory is kept alive and passed on, or others whose descendants culturally honor their memory without letting it fade? What is being remembered in these instances? The whole person or only selected moments, experiences, accomplishments? Surely the latter. So whatever immortality we can bestow on others is at best temporary and partial.

The same is not true for God. As chapter one pointed out, God relates to everyone and everything fully. God has a perfect, complete relation to everyone who lives. In the case of the wife, God knows her actual existence fully, more fully than she herself. God relates to her in all her relationships and keeps them alive in God's awareness or experience. To speak in human terms, if God wanted to, God could reenact her whole life once it has been lived. Would God want to do such a thing?

The answer seems to be, yes. Why? In order to give back to us what we originally gave God—our experience, our concrete existence, our selves, except that in this return gift, there is something new. During her lifetime, the wife's experience was primarily an experience of her selfhood. This does not mean she was selfish or doted on her own feelings. It simply means that she was an acting, feeling, thinking subject. She was the center of her existence. Otherwise, she wouldn't have been a person at all but a certain amount of energy or matter that would have been part of the total world but in no sense identifiable as this woman.

To be a subject is to be centered, to have a core of experience from which to relate to anything else. This core or center *is* one's selfhood. As relationships change, the experience of oneself changes, but throughout there is a centering core that remains our selfhood. We recognize this process in stages of development, maturity, crisis, transition, etc. Relationships weave in and around ourself, constituting our actual existence. Everything that a person, like the wife, is in relation to is experienced as happening *to her*. In one very real sense, the whole world pivots around her; the way she experiences that world *is* her existence, her life, her selfhood. This is not by choice or an option; it is the nature of life in a relational world.

Now, according to what was stated in chapter one, the way the wife experienced her world, i.e., the world as centered around her, is a contribution to God and through God to others. It is a contribution because it is a unique experience of the world that only this woman will generate, and so it adds to God's total experience or relationship. This is what God gives back to us—our experience, our selves *as God* experiences us. This is the radically new element that God provides, that God alone can provide, and that gives us immortality because nothing in God's experience ever fades or weakens or disappears.

So in answer to the first question about immortality—does it exist—a relational view would answer: If it does, it's only because of God. This may seem evasive. It is, insofar as our own desire for immortality dominates the question. But insofar as the primacy of God dominates, the answer is very clear and emphatic. God alone is responsible for immortality because God alone knows our actual selves so perfectly that God could reenact it and give it back to us. If God were to do so, what would that experience be like?

It would be the exact reverse of the experience a person, like the wife, had while alive. While alive, her experience was centered around her selfhood. The world existed for her insofar as it provided the material out of which she fashioned her relationships. And those relationships are who she is. Now that she has finally become who she is, her actual life is for the world—or more accurately, for God and through God for the world. During her life, she could never experience herself in this way because to be living is to be the center of her own existence. So for the first time she can experience herself as only for others. This may also be described as a feeling of being-with others as they continue to experience their world (including her) for themselves.

Seen in this way, there is a radically new relationship established after the wife's death. It is a relationship that is possible, in its full sense, *only* after her death. If she is freed from anything through death, it is not the world as such, as the Greeks thought. It is the direction of her relationship to the world. Instead of the world being for her, she is now for the world. And she is for the world not as an element like any other (as one atom is like every other atom), but she is for the world precisely in her unique, actual, finalized experience. She cannot know what this is, but God does and that is what God gives back to us, something we cannot give ourselves. The reversal of relationship does not change her final experience of herself but situates it differently—not in the particular series of occasions that constituted *her* life but in the ongoing mixture of occasions that constitutes others' lives.

The reversal of relationship cannot be accomplished by the wife or by anyone else except God. Both God and others, however, have different contributions to make once the relationship has been reversed. God gives the wife back to herself as a whole because only God has experienced her as a whole. Others give her back to herself concretely, in particular, definite aspects because that is how they experienced her. God, of course, also knows what this experience is because God experiences everything and everyone fully. But because these concrete, actual experiences were initially generated in relation to particular persons, those persons can more effectively give them back to the wife. Thus, the particular feelings of her husband for her, what it is about her that especially delights him, how he would feel when she was around—these types of experiences are brought into greater relief and intensified *within the whole* that God alone can give back to her. In this way, through God and others, the wife experiences herself anew; she has a radically new relation to the world; and she becomes immortal because God constantly reenacts her life experience even if others do not.

From this perspective, it is clear that her immortal life has a connection with this life. What that connection is, including the possibility of reunion with her husband when he dies, will be explained more fully in chapter five. Underlying this whole relational view is the conviction that everything is always related to everything else. The form of the relationship may alter, even radically; the quality or level of the experience in the relationship may change, even radically; but everything is interrelated or interdependent.

The foregoing is admittedly speculative. It seeks to be consistent with a relational view of life and to affirm what our faith reveals. In summary, we can say that an afterlife is not automatic or necessary or natural. It requires a special act of God. That act is manifested in the life of Jesus. What is described biblically as the resurrection may also be described as a radical reversal of a person's relationship to the world. Instead of the world being for us, death enables us to be for the world, and God gives us back to ourselves in this radically reversed relationship. In doing so, God gives us back to ourselves as a whole, while those we related to in life give us back to ourselves concretely and specifically.

In this whole explanation, God is the primary and indispensable factor. Without God, most of our experience would simply be lost once it had occurred. Without God, there would be no possibility of genuine immortality. Without God, there would be no lasting connection between this life and the afterlife. If this is true as presented in the theological reflection above, does it shed any light on the husband's experience and questions?

Practical Implication

The husband's dominant feeling after the funeral was a new presence of his wife to him. He didn't expect that and wasn't sure if it was real or his imagination. Such an experience leads directly to the relational explanation offered above. From that perspective, when his wife died, he should have expected to feel her presence in a new way because she is in a new relationship to him. Death enables her to become fully for him (and others). This does not mean she wasn't for him during her life. It means that while she lived, *she* was necessarily the organizing, unifying center of her life. From *that* indispensable core of her own becoming, she could be for him. Now that her becoming has ceased, she can be for him totally. Whatever that is specifically, he is feeling it both as real and as new.

There is another important aspect to this new experience. It is ultimately made possible by God's gracious power to bestow immortality. If the husband is experiencing his wife now as immortal, it is because of God. But God's causality in such an event is not external, remote, or predestined. It is like everything else in this view: relational, present, intimate. So, the husband is experiencing not just his wife in a new way but God as well, and he experiences God in a new way *because* his wife's death, immortality, and presence are made possible only by God's relational activity.

Finally, it could be suggested to the husband that his experience of his wife is not just receptive. His reaffirmation of her, his memory and feeling for her, his reenacting her presence is also a contribution to her immortal experience. He gives her back to herself in many specific, concrete ways, all of which let her know what she contributes to him. This knowledge is not like acquiring new information, which is characteristic of life before death. Instead it is a sense or feeling of what she has become for him. Without him, she would not know that concretely. And without God, she wouldn't even be.

·4·

A Sister's Cremation

The Question of Resurrection

Experience

It is a weekday morning. A woman in her late fifties is knocking hard and loud on her neighbor's door. The neighbor is only a few years older than her friend, but she recently had a foot operation and still moves around rather slowly. Besides, her hearing is a little impaired and her doorbell never works. Her friend knows all this, so she makes a lot of noise when she comes by and waits for the door to open.

Usually she and her neighbor do things together: go to church, shop, play cards, watch TV. They are both widows and have been close friends most of their adult lives. They find mutual support in their friendship and they look out for each other. In fact, this recent foot operation was a joint decision. It was corrective surgery that didn't have to be done but was supposed to help relieve some discomfort. They talked about it, considered the implications, inquired about medical coverage and costs, and finally decided to go ahead with it.

Their shared feeling was that even though they were aging and "past their prime," there was no reason why they shouldn't take good care of themselves. If minor foot surgery would make it easier and more comfortable for one of them to get around and there were no real obstacles, why not do it? Part of their agreement was that while the one was recuperating, the other would do the shopping for her, pay her bills at the bank (to save on postage), cash her pension check, etc. They had it all worked out and things had been going well the first week after the operation.

When the door finally opened, it was obvious something was wrong. As the one woman inched back on her cane into the house, she kept grumbling and complaining. She was very disturbed about something. It took a few minutes to calm her down and get the story. Late last night she had received a phone call from her brother-in-law telling her that her sister had died. That was shocking enough, but when she asked about the funeral arrangements, she was told that her sister had already been cremated. That disturbed her most of all.

The news of her sister's death was quite surprising. She had been in reasonably good health for someone nearing sixty-five. On the other hand, she didn't write or phone very often, and she had been living in a city 300 miles away, so visits were infrequent. Anything could have been happening to her health and the family wouldn't have known about it unless she took the trouble to tell them. Her husband surely wouldn't.

He had never been on good terms with the rest of the family. They all felt he had seduced their sister and caused her to divorce her first husband whom they all loved. Sometimes they felt angry toward the sister; sometimes they felt sorry for her. She didn't seem to be all that happy in her second marriage, almost as if she were being controlled by her husband. There was never much variation in the family's feelings toward him; they were always angry with him.

Another reason why they couldn't stand him was that he was an avowed agnostic. He made no secret of his disregard for religion and seemed (to the family) to delight in criticizing church-going people as hypocrites or duty-bound slaves to habit. He could be very cynical about religious beliefs and practices, all of which the family valued very highly. They were staunch, traditional Christians who were very involved in the church and very dependable volunteers.

Over the years a lot of hostility built up and was never dealt with directly or honestly. Everyone seemed content to tolerate the husband on the occasional visits home (no one ever visited *them*) and to communicate only with their sister. So it was quite strange to hear his voice on the phone last night. The conversation was not lengthy. He simply wanted to inform the family that their sister (he did not say his wife) had died and in accordance with her wishes had been cremated. Her ashes were in a mausoleum. Settlement of the estate would be handled soon, but almost everything had been willed to the husband.

The call had come too late for the sister to let her neighbor know, but she launched right in as soon as she came to the door. She had a mixture of feelings: sadness that her sister had died, frustration that she couldn't have seen her and didn't even know that she had been ill, anger at the husband for not telling anyone, and outrage at the fact that her sister had been cremated. She kept lamenting that "she had to have something like that done to her." It seemed just like her husband to pull such a thing, knowing how it would disturb everyone in the family. And cremation! Here she was, going through this operation at her age to try to feel her best and take care of herself, because she was always taught that our bodies are the temple of the Holy Spirit and we should take care of them. Her sister knew that too, and now she was cremated.

It didn't help when her friend tried to point out that she was just as dead whether cremated or embalmed. To her sister, she had been violated. Maybe pagans who don't worship the true God and don't know any better can cremate people. But in this case, someone had intruded into the way God intends things to be done. And she knew just who that someone was and why he had done it.

Theological Question

The sister in this instance doesn't seem to have any questions. She is full of judgments and feelings built up over years of pent-up animosity. Very little that anyone can say or do now will change that. But underneath her anger, there are two issues that may be troublesome to her and that are real questions for other people. One concerns our bodily existence and its value in our ultimate destiny. The other is the actual condition of our bodily selves in the afterlife, what has customarily been referred to as the resurrection of the body.

This woman places real value on her own bodily existence. She is willing to go through an unpleasant operation to improve her physical condition, and she seemed to feel some theological responsibility for taking care of herself, symbolized in the notion that she is a temple of the Holy Spirit. The value of the body is largely shared by people, whether from religious motives or not. The only self we know is a bodily self, and so we are prone to affirm our bodiliness as good because it is who we are. The question is whether this value, which seems so clear in this life, carries over to the next life. Is our bodiliness valuable enough to be included in our immortal existence?

Opinions divide on this question. As we saw in the previous chapter, the Greek philosophical tradition, which has influenced our Christian theology so much, did not see the body as valuable enough to carry over to the immortality of the soul. In fact, the body was seen as a liability to the soul, no matter how useful or necessary it might be for existence in this life. The body simply belongs to a lower level of existence, and the sooner it can be discarded, the better. This leads to a dualistic view that many still espouse, according to which the material and spiritual, body and soul, are seen as separate and unequal elements, temporarily joined together (during our lifetime) but separated in death so that the soul can assume its rightful, higher place. The body has some pragmatic value for life in this world, but no value whatsoever for the afterlife.

The Jewish tradition, which has also influenced Christian theology, although not always so much as the Greek philosophical tradition, did see the body as valuable and integral to the life of the person. This was felt so strongly that for a long time Jewish people envisioned no immortality or resurrection for the dead because it seemed to them that when death occurred, the whole person died. Death meant a kind of hazy, indefinite drowziness, not exactly unconsiousness but certainly not fully alert, active existence. This conclusion followed from their very holistic view, which many people today espouse on different grounds, according to which the material and the spiritual, the body and soul, are inseparably united. Whatever the fate of one, that is the fate of the other. Bodysoul existence is always a united, integral existence.

The Jewish expectation of a general resurrection, which had been developing shortly before the time of Jesus, was consistent with this holistic view. At the end time, the dead would be raised up by God. The whole, bodysoul person would be resurrected. This expectation, and the language/imagery used to convey it, was used by the early Jewish Christians to express their experience that Jesus had been raised from death by God. One of the startling features of their proclamation was that one person had been resurrected before the rest. But another feature was not so startling to Jewish hearers: Jesus had been raised as a bodysoul person.

Many persons today accept a holistic view of the human person not on biblical grounds but on modern scientific, biological, psychological grounds. On this basis alone, many persons conclude, like the ancient Jews, that the whole person dies. Without any religious belief in immortality or resurrection to supplement this conviction, they see nothing beyond this life. There are no compelling reasons to think that one part of a person lives on if the whole person does not live on, and it is hard to imagine how a whole bodysoul person can live on.

Perhaps the cremated sister's husband felt this way. He just didn't have any persuasive reason to think that the whole person who is his wife doesn't die completely. The traditional religious beliefs of his in-law family may have struck him as a hodgepodge of philosophy and religion with no real consistency. His wife dies; her body decays but the soul lives on; eventually the body will be resurrected and reunited with the soul. His wife will be complete again. But what about in the meantime? Was she whole or not? Either the body is integral to a person's existence or it isn't. If it isn't, why reunite it? If it is, how can it be suspended and the person still be in existence? The attempt to have it both ways strikes many people today as inconsistent and possibly unnecessary. The real task is to explain the immortality of the whole person without minimizing the value of the body dimension by postponing its inclusion or presenting it as an eventual additon to the *real* person, the soul.

This touches on the second theological issue lying behind the irate sister's feelings—the resurrection of the body. The resurrection of the body certainly points to the ultimate value of the body, the material dimension of afterlife, and sees the whole person as the ultimate goal. But the resurrection, as pointed out in the last chapter, is a special act of God. It is not an automatic, natural event. This fact alone may make some people wonder how intrinsically related the body is to the soul if it takes a special act of God to resurrect it. However, if we do not assume the Greek idea of a temporary separation of body and soul, then we can think of the resurrection as affecting the whole person, all at once—as the ancient Jews thought of it. When this holistic resurrection takes place is another matter, one we shall discuss shortly.

Apart from these considerations, there is the further question of what the resurrected bodysoul person is like. Usually this question is asked in terms of the body only, because it is assumed (from the Greeks again) that the soul is what it is and cannot be different, whereas the body, or our bodiliness, can take different forms. This is part of the sister's anxiety about cremation. What if something essential to the bodily composition is destroyed in that act? What if our resurrected body depends in some way on the condition of our body when we die?

Speculation about what the resurrected body is like has virtually nothing to go on. The accounts of Jesus' resurrected appearances are highly stylized proclamations that do not seem to have been written to give us information for *our* questions. Probably the response of St. Paul to the Christians in Corinth is the most perceptive (1 Cor. 15:35–36). When asked what sort of body the dead will have when they are raised, he replied that that was a foolish question.

Well, foolish or not, theology tries to answer it, speculatively but consistently with what is known from tradition as well as what is seen, maybe for the first time, in contemporary experience. The challenge to theology is to affirm the whole person while explaining the resurrection. How does theology do this?

Theological Reflection

A typical theology keeps the discussion of the resurrection of the body in its proper biblical context—the resurrection of the dead. To isolate discussion and focus it on the body is a misleading theological direction. The resurrection of the dead conveys two important points. One is the whole person; the other is the communal or social aspect of resurrection.

Death affects the whole person, not just the body. It is incorrect, from a theological point of view, to say that only our body dies. The thorough, permeating dimension of death is better conveyed by the expression resurrection of the dead, which is also the biblical and early creedal expression. This is hard for many people to grasp today because we have become so accustomed to thinking of death as a separation of body and soul, implying that the soul is unaffected by death. But if the soul is embodied, indeed if the purpose of the human soul is to enliven bodily matter, then even a separation is a death for the soul in the sense that its purpose is over, its capacity to enliven this body is completed, its existence as an integral part of *this* bodysoul person is terminated.

In addition, the phrase "the dead" is a collective. It includes all those who have died. Whether we assume that each of us is essentially an individual who chooses to join others in various forms of social grouping or that each of us is primarily and inescapably social, the fact remains that death is a shared experience that ironically unites or confirms us in some social dimension. Consistent with this, resurrection conveys a social or communal event, the raising up of *those* who have died.

Given this holistic and communal dimension, a typical theology cannot say much beyond the fact that our bodies will be transformed through the resurrection. This event is generally associated with the end of the world but not much more is specified. For the most part, the biblical imagery of the end time is retained and the philosophical description of immortality (sketched in the previous chapter) is used. The two are put together without a great deal of harmony, and the questions of the cremated woman's sister are not often dealt with. The result is a not very satisfying explanation of the resurrection of the body in the context of the resurrection of the dead.

Some modern theologians, relying on insights and suggestions from human development studies, have tried to describe a kind of total human process that goes on in and during the experience of death. In these descriptions, the person (e.g., the cremated sister) acts as the primary agent, finally shaping her whole life project and emerging as a whole into an immortal, afterlife state. Viewed from an immortal perspective (God's), this could be called a kind of resurrection or transition from one form of bodysoul life to a new form of bodysoul life. The resurrection in this sense would occur at death rather than in some future time. The communal dimension is expressed in the fact that who she finally becomes is influenced by and includes all the others who have been part of her life in any significant way.

This approach appeals to many people, although it does not seem to do complete justice to the biblical accounts/expectations of the resurrection of the dead, and it seems to minimize God's active role in the process. It cannot really be called a typical theology of resurrection because not that many theologians today advocate such a view, but it is a new explanation that tries to answer consistently the questions raised above. Such a view draws upon a relational understanding of reality and will be developed more fully later.

One of the goals of a typical theology of resurrection is to affirm the value and dignity of the body, even if we don't know very clearly what happens or will happen to it in the resurrection of the dead. One of the most concrete ways this value and dignity is expressed is by the reverence/care shown for the corpse. *How* this is expressed will vary from culture to culture, or from time to time within a given culture. The customary practice in our society of embalming and publicly viewing the body is one way of doing this, but it is by no means the only way. Variations from the customary practice, however, are sometimes interpreted as a variation from the underlying value. That seems to be the case with the sister. She interpreted her sister's cremation as a violation of her dignity.

She may have had other concerns, depending on how literally she understood the resurrection of the body to be a raising of *this* bodily material. Of course, for someone who believes that God can and does create out of nothing, recreating or reconstituting the ashes of a person would not seem to be that much of a problem. This degree of literal belief, however, does pose another, real problem because it tends to equate resurrection with resuscitation and perhaps to overidentify the resurrection with what happens to the body. When people make this identification, they lose sight of the faith proclamation about resurrection and reduce this great and hopeful mystery to a problem of chemistry and biology.

Respect is shown to the corpse, not necessarily because this body will be enlivened again one day to function more or less as it did during the sister's lifetime, but because the sister's bodiliness, concretized in and through *this* body, remains an inseparable dimension of her very existence. We can't relate as directly or intimately to her existence now as we used to, but her corpse (or ashes) gives us some point of contact, some focus for our attention. It is no longer who she *is*, but it is a reminder of who she *was*. Whatever transformation has taken place or will take place in her existence, it is a transformation of an actual life that this corpse was integrally part of as her earthly body. It is that past and future *life* which is valued, and this is expressed by showing respect to the corpse.

These points fit in with a relational view of reality and can be amplified by looking more closely at that view and asking: How would the resurrection of the body be interpreted in a relational approach?

The foundation for a relational interpretation is the relation of the body and the soul. Other terms could be used to describe these two primary dimensions of human existence and experience, but these are the customary ones. In the last chapter, the husband's new experience of his wife's presence was explained as a radical new relationship that she had assumed to the world through death. Instead of the world being for her, she was now for the world. It was mentioned that during her lifetime, she was the center of her existence and the world provided her with the material out of which she created her relationships, i.e., who she was to be, her selfhood.

In a relational view, this pattern is found in everything that is actual. But the actual things we know most about are ourselves as human beings. Our experience of being alive is an experience of centering the world around us, of bringing the world into relationship with us, from our perspective. We cannot *not* do this and be alive. Now, the organizing, coordinating center of our existence is our selfhood or soul. This has two dimensions. One is the general nature or character of the human soul. Whatever it is that makes the human soul human and distinct from all other life-centering forces, *that* is the general nature of the soul.

But this general soul never actually exists except in relationships because nothing is actual unless it is in relation. So the soul is human at one level and simultaneously personal or self at another level. The second level is the level of concrete experiences, of particular occasions of relationship. Thus, in a relational view, there is no such thing as an unrelated human soul or a soul related only in general to the world. Actually to *be* a human soul, it has to be in relationship concretely, specifically.

Obviously, this understanding is in conflict with the classic Greek notion that the soul could and should escape its relation to the body and exist body-less in a totally spiritual realm. Such a view is neither possible nor desirable from a thorough and consistent relational perspective.

It is the concrete relationships of the soul that are of initial interest here and that are most accessible to us. The nature of the soul as such is known to us only through these concrete relationships since that is the only way we know anything. And the most significant soul relationship is the relation to the body. The body is the immediate environment of the soul, the physical point of contact with the available material world. How this intimate relationship originates is not the prime concern here but rather how the soul and body function together. They function in an interdependent way.

This means that they provide something indispensable for each other (just as the world provides God with actual experiences and God provides the world with ranked possibilities from those experiences). The body provides the soul with concrete, limited, definite, specific material to relate to; the soul provides the body with order, direction, harmony, coordination. The body's contribution to the soul comes in numerous ways, through sensations, impulses, perceptions, location, etc., all of which are filtered through the brain. The soul's contribution to the body comes in numerous ways also, through memory, judgment, intuition, imagination, etc., all of which are filtered through the brain. In this sense, the brain is the meeting place of the soul and body.

These interactions occur so rapidly that we are not aware of most of them. We become aware only of large-scale, dominant, and relatively final impressions. Our feelings, our thoughts, our movements, our sensory perceptions—each of these is itself a clustering of innumerable interactions between the soul and the body exchanged through the brain. In all of this activity, the soul is constantly relating to, experiencing the body as *its* body, and the body is sensing the world as a world for *its* soul. There is an intimate "withness" that characterizes the relationship.

This may be detected by the way we speak of ourselves as acting. We do not say that we see what our eyes see or hear what our ears hear, as if our experience and the organs of our experience were separate. We say that we see *with* our eyes or *our* eyes see; we hear with our ears or our ears hear. Our language is accurate. We are verbalizing one of our most basic, intimate, complex experiences, and because it is so close to us, because it *is* our self experiencing, we tend not to be aware of it.

One of the implications of this view is that in every occasion of experience the soul and body are experiencing together. They do not experience the same thing together, but they experience themselves being together; they experience their intimate interdependence. This experience is repeated countless times in every instant, but each time is new and reinforces all the previous times while opening up into the next time. Until death.

At death this interdependent activity ceases. Whatever causes the cessation, the result is that the bodysoul interrelationship ends. Does anything remain? Yes, and this is where the general nature or character of the soul comes in. What remains is the accumulation of previous bodysoul experiences. This accumulation is housed in the soul because the soul has a capacity for order, coordination, harmony, synthesis, etc. This is characteristic of the soul, whereas the body is an ordered, coordinated, harmonized vehicle for supplying the "stuff" of experience. The body in this active respect does not remain after death; it becomes a corpse. But the body, in the sense of the intimate supplier of the soul with the primary data of its experiences, remains with the soul.

To translate this into somewhat more concrete terms: the cremated wife's life consisted of innumerable relationships or experiences. In each one, her bodysoul was the way she experienced; indeed, she was her bodysoul experiences. This means her experience was what her soul (self) experienced of the world her body provided. Put another way, her soul experienced the world that was her body, the world mediated by her body. These experiences were the relationships that constituted her life, and every one of those experiences included a bodysoul relationship.

How does this relate to the resurrection of the body? Initially, it means that the body that is resurrected is the body as experienced in the lifetime of bodysoul relationships to the world. This bodily experience is not *every* occasion that was shared by the bodysoul. It is rather those occasions that the soul retains, reaffirms, includes, remembers, etc. Put another way, the resurrected body is the relevant body in the soul's experience.

This is the unity, the wholeness, the integral and inseparable oneness that has been affirmed in the biblical tradition. This is the only actual body there is, and it shares in the destiny of the soul after death. The material construct that was the active body before death is now the corpse, no longer actually related to the bodysoul person who has died, and no longer relevant to the future (immortal) bodysoul experience.

In this view, the resurrection of the body is immediate, and the soul is the prime agent. Through the experience of relating to the body, which is an accumulated experience, the soul preserves the body as an integral part of its own experience. The soul could not eliminate this experience and still be the soul because the body is too intimately and integrally part-of the experiences that constitute the soul. The unity is unbreakable, but is it immortal?

The bodysoul experience just described is the initial moment or phase of the resurrection of the body. It is the foundation for the next moment or phase of resurrection, that provided by God. As mentioned previously, God relates to everything and everyone that is actual. The bodysoul experience after death is an actual experience that God relates to fully. In this act of relating, God keeps the bodysoul experience actual, in existence, and does so in the way described in the previous chapters.

But more than this, God relates this "resurrected" bodysoul to all the other experiences that God relates to, including in this comprehensive network all those who have previously died. In the terminology being used here, God relates each resurrected bodysoul person to every other resurrected bodysoul person. This is something only God can do. The soul of each person can resurrect the body of that person through the accumulated, uniquely intimate relationship generated through a lifetime; God resurrects that same bodysoul person by including it in the accumulating, uniquely comprehensive relationship generated by God's experience.

This is not just an addition to the bodysoul resurrection. Without God's inclusion, the bodysoul experience could not survive. It would be neither immortal nor resurrected in the full sense of the general resurrection of the dead. Only *that* resurrection endures, and only that resurrection is God's to effect. In this way, a relational view affirms both God's primacy and the resurrection of the dead, not just the resurrection of the body. In fact, the resurrection of the body would be only a momentary experience, passing out of actuality almost as soon as it became actual unless there were a resurrection of the dead to sustain it. And only God can resurrect the dead.

In this view, however, the resurrection of the dead is an ongoing, ever-increasing event. There is no real interim state between a person's death and the final resurrection. There is a continual process of inserting each person with his or her personal bodysoul resurrection into the accumulation of others who have died and are given immortality by God. This seems consistent with a relational view, but is it consistent with our belief? The full answer to that question can only be given by looking at the next two chapters on judgment and the end of the world.

At this point, it is sufficient to note the following. In this approach, the unity of the human person is maintained. This means that the value of the bodily dimension is upheld. Moreover, that value carries over to immortality, while the unity of the bodysoul person is simultaneously affirmed by explaining more carefully in what sense the body is united to the soul and remains united after death. Finally, the resurrection of the body is integrally related to the resurrection of the dead as God's act whereby each individual is related to all others through God's relational experience. Thus, at bottom everything of ultimate value derives from God, which is what any theology aims at proclaiming.

Practical Implication

In the case that began this chapter, the sister was disturbed that her sister had been cremated. According to the theological reflection developed here, there is no need to be disturbed. She might have other concerns, especially relative to her sister's husband, but cremation itself does not affect the eventual resurrection of her sister. Her ashes have a value as a concrete focal point for those who knew her, but the resurrection of the body doesn't pertain to this remnant as such. This may not be easy to explain to the sister, especially if her own convictions are tied in with a very literal reading of Scripture. Probably the most effective way to communicate with her is to invoke God's power to raise up her sister. The relational view presented here affirms the same thing but explains it quite differently. If a further explanation were needed (or if she could really hear it), it would follow along the line presented above. The key points are that we live and die as whole persons and we are raised to immortal life by God alone along with the rest of the dead.

Part of her disturbance over the cremation also stems from her own valuation of the body and the care she takes of hers. These values are worth affirming. From a relational point of view, the body *is* important; in fact, it is indispensable. The body is not just an instrument, used rather mechanically to get on in life until we are freed from its restrictions. The body is how we relate to the world, and the quality of our relating is partly dependent on the condition of our bodiliness. This important role of the body generates a respect for it, both in life and in death, but cremation isn't necessarily a sign of disrespect.

More than anything else, questions about resurrection should lead to a reaffirmation and clarity about the primacy of God. No matter how we understand or explain resurrection, we can't resurrect ourselves. Only God can do so, and God does so only in relation to everyone else, i.e., the resurrection of the dead. God seems willing to do this; in fact, God virtually needs to do so to be true to the divine nature of relating to everyone and everything fully. Not to resurrect someone would be to let that person simply die, pass into oblivion. This would diminish God's perfection or fullness because there would be one less relationship than there could have been. This seems to suggest that no one is every excluded from God's relationship. That has direct implications for the next topic: judgment.

5

A Brother's Suicide
The Question of Judgment

Experience

It had been a hard day for the minister, this third day of a week-long retreat. He had looked forward to this week as a break away from his hectic parish schedule. He had felt the need to stop for a while and reflect on what he had been doing in his ministry, what it meant to him, and where it seemed to be leading him. But instead of a relaxing and peaceful review of his life, he found himself facing questions he could more easily avoid in the active ministry: Was this really a valuable service to others? Was he just giving people what they wanted, or was he challenging them, helping them to grow and mature in their faith? Was *he* growing? Did he feel really close to anyone, or was his work consuming him?

He was mulling over these things after dinner when word came that the parish deacon was there to see him. He could think only that something had happened in the parish because the deacon was covering for him while he was away. Typical, he thought, even when you try to take some time off, something always comes up that only *you* can handle. He felt the parish and his ministry tightening in on him as he went to the front of the retreat house. What the deacon had come to tell him was that the minister's younger brother had committed suicide.

The brothers came from a family of four boys. Their father worked two jobs and their mother was often ill. She had to be taken care of by the children more often than she could take care of them. As a result, the boys grew up to be very self-reliant and independent. They didn't experience a great deal of personal attention or favor from either parent. The boys' determination paid off. The oldest son excelled in school and won a full college scholarship. His success put pressure on the rest of the boys to do likewise.

After high school and a couple of years working, the next son decided he would enter the ministry. In his family such a choice was highly valued because they were very devout Christians and tried to live faithful, hard-working, humble lives. Everyone was very proud of him and reinforced his decision all through the seminary years. Everyone except his younger brother, but then he seemed to react against all his brothers. He did not do well in school; he couldn't keep a job; and he didn't seem to want to. He had some friends but none of the relationships lasted. Now in his mid-twenties, he had been drinking more and more and was suspected of getting into drugs as well.

The minister-brother felt a special responsibility toward him. After all, he had dedicated his life to helping people in crisis, and he had acquired both skill and experience in doing so. And yet, it was more difficult to approach his own brother. He didn't want to invade his privacy, and he didn't want to come on as a moralizing clergyman. If the truth be told, he really didn't know what to say anyhow. Most of the things he heard himself saying when he imagined talking to his brother felt like artificial piety or religious jargon. You ought to have a purpose in your life; God has a destiny or plan for each of us; you don't do yourself or anyone else a favor by taking drugs; you're a good person with many gifts. . . .

Imagining himself saying those things made the minister-brother realize how much he had been resisting, sometimes even rejecting, the typical style of ministry he had been trained in. He wondered if he was also rejecting the Christian way or style of life. The two were so closely connected for him, and he was not sure where he stood with either one right now. So he hesitated to speak to his brother because he wasn't sure he could be helpful, and he might have to face some things in his own life that he would rather avoid.

Recognizing all this, he decided to make this retreat. He felt it would give him the chance to sort out his feelings, to claim what he saw as valid and meaningful and leave the rest aside. That might even mean leaving the ministry altogether and he was prepared for that. He was prepared for just about anything except the news of his brother's suicide.

The deacon sat with him while the minister tried to sort through his reactions. He couldn't believe that his brother felt so badly about himself. He asked the deacon if he was sure it was suicide; maybe he had accidentally overdosed if he were using drugs. There was no accident. The brother had left a clear suicide note explaining that he could not find any purpose in his life to keep going. He knew he was troublesome to others; so why make or keep everybody unhappy? The shock of the news alternated with strong feelings of guilt. The minister kept asking himself why he didn't recognize that his brother was so bad off. Did his preoccupation with his own ministerial crisis blind him to the signals his brother was sending? He knew from his training and from some occasional experience that people inclining to suicide usually give indications before they act. Why didn't someone pick them up in this case? Why didn't *he*?

His feelings of guilt made him aware again of how responsible we are for one another and how much we depend on one another for support, guidance, truth, purpose. He knew he was in need of some reinforcement in his ministry, and he looked to others to provide it; but he seemed to miss his brother's need, or if he sensed it, he didn't respond adequately. It made him feel very fragile and helpless.

His thoughts also turned to God and especially to how God would judge his brother. He never did believe that God was a stern, demanding judge who would punish people if their wrongs deserved it. (One of the views discussed in chapter two.) On the other hand, to take his own life, the brother had to feel pretty worthless. Had he rejected God? Did he turn his back on the opportunities God may have offered him to find meaning? His suicide was deliberate, a choice he had made. How responsible was he for that choice? How accountable before God? Just then the minister realized that he'd better head for home.

Theological Question

As the minister reflected on his feelings about his brother's suicide, two thoughts kept recurring: our responsibility for one another and God's judgment of how well we fulfill that responsibility. People who believe in immortality may think about God's judgment when any death occurs. It's part of the unknown dimension of death that makes us suspenseful, nervous, anxious, fearful. But a suicide makes us aware, in a way that other death experiences don't, how interdependent we are. Like it or not, we are tied in with each other and we affect the way another person lives—and dies.

This responsibility moves between two extremes. At one extreme each person is considered solely responsible for every choice, action, decision, etc., that is made. This attitude presupposes a very self-contained, isolated, almost stoic understanding of the human person and works against any involvement or influence from outside the person as through family, church, society. On this end of the spectrum, there is not much chance for community or sharing or relationship.

At the other extreme no one has much personal responsibility for what happens. Indeed, individuals aren't allowed to make personal choices or decisions. The community or church or society predetermines everything. Individuals are one with the larger group; their identity coincides with the identity of the whole. Everyone is responsible and no one is responsible.

Most people find themselves between these two extremes. There are shaping influences from outside of us that minimize our responsibility, either for ourselves or for others. We cannot usurp another person's responsibility for self-direction. While no one of us is completely autonomous, neither are we completely determined. In the realm of *inter*action, *inter*relation, *inter*dependence, we face the difficult question: How responsible are we for one another, not in the abstract, but in the concrete, with this person, for this action or decision?

Our ambiguity oftentimes about our responsibility gives greater weight to God's judgment. Presumably, God is not ambiguous. God knows exactly what our responsiblity is in every situation. Maybe we should have known more clearly too. Or maybe we were very clear but wrong. How understanding is God? And how merciful? If we have shirked our responsibility, if we have simply not developed our sense of responsibility, if we have failed to carry it out fully, what will happen? What will God do about it?

So the question of God's judgment ultimately is, for us, a question of reward and punishment. If there were no personal outcome, we wouldn't care that much what God's judgment is. Or if we felt that everything would be worked out in this life, we could expect to "get what we deserve," and we would have a pretty good idea what that would be in terms of human experience in this life. But things don't seem to work out completely in this life. Too many good and innocent people suffer while too many dishonest and selfish people get what they want. These observations, coupled with a belief in immortality, give rise to the expectation that right and wrong, responsibility and irresponsibility will finally be taken care of in the next life. And that means that God's judgment has everlasting effects.

For some, this prospect is a major stimulus for the way they live. For others, it has no bearing at all. Underlying either view is a particular understanding of God and how God operates. It is preeminently the task of theology to express our best understanding of God and how God operates in order to clarify what our responsibilities are and what we may expect to happen when we fulfill them and when we don't.

Theological Reflection

A typical theology of judgment presupposes that we are responsible for our actiondecisions. (This strange word is used here to convey the idea that our decisions must be enacted to become actual, and also to avoid looking at actions as isolated acts, apart from the whole context of deciding which produces them.) This in turn presupposes that we are free to act even though our freedom is conditioned by the influence of both limitation and sin (as discussed in chapter two). When we fail to exercise our freedom responsibly, we sin. When this actually is the case and when it is not must be decided through moral discernment. The intent of this reflection is not on deciding when freedom is used responsibly in given instances and when it isn't. The interest is rather in clarifying how

God judges our actiondecisions and what results from that judgment.

A typical theology of judgment affirms that the ultimate judgment of a person's life, like the brother who committed suicide, is made by God, but that God exercises this judgment through Jesus. This is part of what is implied in the title, Jesus as Lord. To be Lord means that Jesus is the embodiment, the fulfillment, the perfection of God's relationship in human life. Because of this, Jesus as Lord is the norm by which everyone else is judged, for we are all meant to be as fully the embodiment, the fulfillment, the perfection of God's relationship in our human life as Jesus was in his. None of us can be more perfect than Jesus; therefore, Jesus is the standard by which our perfection is measured.

Typically, theology tries to express this by drawing upon both philosophical and biblical sources, just as it does when explaining immortality and resurrection. Corresponding to the immortality of the soul, as depicted by the Greek philosophers, there is a particular judgment immediately after death. Because of the image of the soul leaving the body,this judgment seems to be a judgment of the soul only. And yet, it is the final, unchanging, everlasting judgment rendered by God through Jesus as Lord. Presumably, the soul enters the state it is judged worthy of, even though the body is yet to be resurrected and reunited with it.

Corresponding to the resurrection of the dead, as depicted graphically by the Jewish Scriptures, there is a general judgment at the end of the world. Because of the imagery of resurrection, this judgment clearly appears as a judgment of the whole person and of all persons together. It, too, is final, unchanging, and everlasting, rendered by God through Jesus as Lord, as narrated in Matthew 25:31–46.

Borrowing in this way from these two sources obviously creates some problems. There appear to be two judgments: the particular judgment at the end of each person's life, involving the soul only, and the general judgment at the end of the world, involving the whole person and all people. The latter appears to be a duplication of the former with nothing essentially added to the judgment, although there is the addition of the resurrected body to the soul and the public character to the previous, private judgment. These are not insignificant additions to the *event*, but they do not add to the judgment unless the immediate, particular judgment is incomplete without the general, public judgment. But in that case, what state is the soul in, separated from the body between the particular and general judgment? It would seem more consistent to say with the biblical Jews that the whole person dies and awaits resurrection and judgment.

The heart of the problem is trying to make compatible two different views that really are not compatible. If theology follows the Greek notion consistently, then the body is not included in the afterlife, and trying to find a way to keep the soul in readiness for this reunion just won't work. On the other hand, if theology follows the Jewish notion, the bodysoul is kept in readiness for the final resurrection, but that doesn't seem compatible with our understanding of Jesus' resurrection as an immediate event and its implied promise that we too are united with him when we die. It is clear that theology wants to affirm that each person and all people are judged by God through Jesus as Lord. When and how this takes place is not as clearly worked out when both the philosophical and biblical traditions are put side by side.

In one sense this is not the primary concern with judgment. It is the outcome that counts. Here, typical theology affirms two ultimate possibilities: heaven or hell, with some prospect of an interim state (purgatory) between the time of our death and our full entrance into heaven. For many people today neither the interim state nor hell are taken seriously as possibilities.

The notion of an interim state never did achieve complete acceptance in the church's history and is not widely affirmed at the present time. Partly this is due to the way it has been depicted and partly due to its rationale. The depiction of the interim state as hell-with-an-end strikes most modern people as fanciful. The standard graphic images are not very fearsome and do not constitute the essence of this view in any event. For that reason, some contemporary theologians have tried to recast this notion in terms more compatible with our outlook on life today.

We all experience change through maturation, crisis, choice, accident, etc. Changing from one condition to another is often painful, as when a child goes through adolescence, or when a spouse adjusts to the death or divorce of another, or when adults enter the aging process. Extrapolating from these experiences, some theologians envision our transition from this life to the next as another painful movement. The experience may not be radically unlike those just mentioned. The degree of pain involved depends on our whole past life. We move more or less easily into the afterlife depending on how we moved through our present life: generously or selfishly, inclusive of others or exclusive, open or closed to newness, freely or predetermined. In experiencing this interim movement, we are experiencing the outcome of our lives, and the passage is a kind of purgation or cleansing of the aspects of our lives that in fact keep us from entering fully into God's relationship with us.

In this way, theologians try to preserve the meaning of the interim state without being bound to some of the imagery associated with it in the past. At the same time, they are trying to recover the rationale for the interim state in the first place. That is, we are responsible for what we do in this life. If we don't fulfill our responsibilities now, we will have to later. This was originally proposed in terms of temporal punishment due to sin. Some abusive practices grew up around this notion, and the impression was given that people could buy their own or another's way out of the interim state. Moreover, the whole idea seemed to undercut the universal salvific effect of Jesus (which shall be discussed in chapter seven).

Theologians who are rethinking the interim state are trying to integrate this part of the tradition with insights from modern psychology and human-development studies. If we are responsible for what we do in life, how do *we* compensate for irresponsible actiondecisions? What do *we* do about those acts of irresponsibility that we can't really reverse or can't adequately make up for once they're done? Does God merely overlook them? Are we cut off from heaven forever because of them? Some kind of interim solution would seem called for if these acts are neither to be simply dismissed (which would call into question how responsible/accountable we really are) nor to deny us our destiny forever.

Whether an interim state described in terms of a personal passage, which is more or less easy depending on how responsibly we have lived our lives, is convincing or not is an open question. Certainly the imagery and rationale for such a transitional state is more coherent than the typical understanding of purgatory. In any event, this is an *interim* state. It is the *final* state that people are really concerned about, and many find it hard to take hell seriously. The primary reason for this is trying to understand how an all-good, loving, merciful God could condemn a person to hell forever. A secondary reason is, once again, the imagery often used to depict hell.

A typical theology affirms the *possibility* of hell because it takes with utmost seriousness our freedom to act responsibly or not. This freedom seems to imply that we are free to say yes or no to God. If we say no, that is our choice. And God respects our freedom. Consequently, hell is a logical and necessary implication of freedom. While affirming this point in this way, theology typically hastens to add that there is no certainty that any human being actually is in hell. However it is depicted and however necessary it seems to be as a corollary to our freedom, hell is only a possibility for typical theology—a real possibility, but not necessarily an actualized one. That knowledge is finally God's. But if there is anyone in hell, it is not because God put the person there. God's judgment is only a ratification of the person's actual life. We are not consigned to hell; we choose our way into hell . . . and into heaven.

A typical theology is more assertive about people being in heaven. Some persons are designated as saints by name, and there is a long-standing reference to the communion of saints. That affirmation is very appealing. The description of heaven, however, often is not. Like the general description of immortality in chapter three, heaven as it is usually imaged seems uneventful, abstract, unappealing, boring. The most concrete references are those that are least likely to be real: pearly gates, St. Peter's list, trumpet blasts, angel wings, etc. Even the beatific vision seems rather static, like looking at something bright for all eternity.

To be sure, there are other attempts to describe the *experience* of heaven that are more exciting and draw upon our best human experiences in this life. But so much of our thinking is influenced by the Greek ideals of contemplation, changelessness, spirit, transcendence that we find it hard to imagine heaven in other ways. A relational view can help us do that, and maybe see judgment, responsibility, the interim state, and hell a little differently too.

In a completely relational approach, such as the one being developed in this book, God is involved in everything that happens. As described in chapter one, this means that God knows completely everything and everyone that is actual, e.g., the brother who committed suicide. God's complete knowledge is operative at two levels. God knows everything there is to know about the brother, and God relates that knowledge to everything else that is actual. This twofold knowledge frames the understanding of immortality and resurrection, as presented in chapters three and four. It also grounds the explanation of judgment.

God's judgment is God's perfect knowledge of the brother and of the brother's relationship to everything else God knows. God's knowledge or judgment of the brother is a particular, immediate, personal judgment. It is God's experience of this man both at every moment of his life and as a completed, finalized, definite person at his death. This judgment of God is couched in the context of all the possibilities that the brother had for becoming who he finally turned out to be. As explained earlier, God experiences every event fully and sees in that event all the possibilities that could flow from it for subsequent, continuous experience. When God sees these possibilities, they are ranked from the best to the worst.

God's ranking may be called a valuation. God offers it in various forms of communication and awaits the actual response, in this case of the brother. Whatever the response is, God experiences it completely, draws all the next possibilities from it, ranks them, and offers them for future enactment. The actual response of the brother is more or less compatible or congruent with the ranking God envisioned. God's determination of whether a given response is more or less harmonious with God's valuation may be called an evaluation or judgment.

God's particular judgment is comprised of both the valuation and evaluation. The valuation of possibilities is what God sees and desires for the brother; the evaluation is what the brother actually chooses, including all the particular factors involved in how he chooses and enacts this possibility rather than that one. Two points are worth noting in this explanation. One is that what God wills for each person is ongoing and constantly developing. It is shaped in and by the relationship God has with the brother. What God wills is partly determined by what the brother does. That is, God always wills what is best for the brother *given* the brother's actual development up to that point. Only God always sees what is best, but God sees only what is best relative to actual conditions.

The second point in this view is that God's judgment is inclusive. God relates to everything that is actual. Whatever the brother does, God experiences it as it is. Nothing is rejected or discarded or pushed outside of God's experience. God evaluates it for what it is and for what it can lead to (valuation). One of the attributes of God is that God *can* draw out of every experience and every event some new possibility for life. Obviously, some events yield very little (as we saw in chapter two). God can see, do, feel only what is actually present in any given relationship, but God does see, do, feel *all* that is present. The relative degree of what is present varies, but God's evaluation of it is always inclusive. In this sense, it may also be said to be positive, as long as "positive" covers a range of degrees.

The evaluation of the brother's actiondecisions relative to God's prior valuation of the brother's possibilities expands when it is put in relation to everything else God knows and evaluates. This may be considered as the general judgment. It is general in the sense that God sees the value of this event, the brother's actiondecision, in relation to everything else which is actual, i.e., everything else that has ever happened. It is also general in the sense that this event affects to some degree the general accumulation; it affects it quantitatively by adding one more experience to the whole, and it affects it qualitatively by being the actual experience it is.

Clearly, only God can form this type of general judgment. If we were to speculate, we might say that the brother's actiondecision to commit suicide was not the best possibility God envisioned for him. Nonetheless, it was one possibility that God also envisioned and presumably ranked as the least desirable. The brother is free, however, and once he has actualized his choice, God experiences everything that makes it what it is. From our perspective, it has minimal value and yields minimal possibilities for new experiences. It has a minimum evaluation.

Relative to everything else that has happened, this minimal event may have slightly more value. That is, it is conceivable that some actiondecisions have been worse and contributed less to God's experience and the world's. In that case, the general judgment might yield a different result, and an event with minimal value in itself (i.e., in relation to its own possibilities) might have greater value in relation to the whole. The complete judgment includes both levels.

It should be noted, however, that the general judgment as described here is never absolutely final. As new events occur, their actual experience is added to the whole. The general evaluation or ordering of actual events to one another is constantly changing, both quantitatively and qualitatively. So the general judgment is always all-inclusive and ongoing. This is simply the equivalent notion regarding judgment that we saw in the last chapter regarding general resurrection.

The evaluation, although changing, is always positive. This means that its value (such as it is) can never be decreased or diminished. It can only be increased. If a less valuable experience is added, relative to that, the previous experience is evaluated more highly. If a comparable experience is added, it reinforces what value is already there. And if a more valuable experience is added, it accentuates the value that *is* there in the previous experience; it affirms all that is in that experience even though there is more of value in the new experience. The "more" pertains only to the new experience; it does not give a corresponding "less" to the previous experience.

One further point to note here. God's general judgment includes everything that has already occurred, but this is not confined to those who have died. Every experience in a person's life once the experience occurs is included, even though the person is still living. This has an important implication for the notion of intercession and leads to a discussion of the interim state.

The brother's evaluation relative to his own possibilities is set, but his evaluation relative to everything else is always open to change as long as there are new events occurring that are added to the whole. One source of new events in this case is the minister's feelings and response (actiondecisions) to his brother. If he has negative responses, anger, exclusiveness, etc. (as the woman in the previous chapter), he will not contribute much to the general evaluation of his brother. However, if he is accepting, understanding, caring, then he will contribute more to the general evaluation of his brother.

In the first instance, the brother's own minimal contribution would be reinforced. In the second instance, the brother's minimal contribution would be put in a different relation; whatever its positive value, it would be enhanced, strengthened, affirmed. In terms of the explanation of immortality in chapter three, the minister would be giving the brother back to himself in a way and to a degree that the brother had not himself chosen to do. In this light, the value of praying for the dead, of remembering others positively, of uniting ourselves with one another in the best sense we are aware of, all have real, contributing value. In this same light, we can begin to see how a relational view might interpret the intercessory role of Jesus' earthly life, a topic that will be discussed in chapter seven.

Does the same type of influence work the other way? Do those who have died intercede for the living, as the grandmother in chapter one expected to do? This is more difficult to affirm in a relational view because those who have died do not generate new events. And yet, in terms of the explanation of immortality in chapter three, after death a person exists for the world. What does this mean? God derives new possibilities from the actual world that has already occurred. Included in that actual world are those who died, with their personal evaluation and (changing) general evaluation. Each new event is a response to possibilities that God offers from the actual world. Usually this means from the actual world most relevant to the new event.

In the case of human persons, those who were directly in relationship with one another while alive would be some of the most relevant sources of new possibilities. Their actual relevance would depend, of course, upon their value in God's total experience. But it is conceivable that the grandmother's life, which had already been a source of possibilities for the couple during their lifetime together, would continue to be so, and perhaps even more so if the grandmother's evaluation in God's general judgment were greater now than when she was alive. In this case, it is *God* who is actively involved mediating the intercession of the grandmother.

This same pattern of influence could be drawn out for other types of relationships: heroes, well-known persons, namesakes, those whose influence is mediated indirectly, patrons, etc. In a relational world, everything is connected, with varying degrees of influence. The actual degree of influence in a given instance depends on God's particular and general evaluation. God's particular evaluation is God's experience of who the person has actually become, relative to the person's possibilities in life; God's general evaluation is God's experience of who the person continues to be, relative to everything else that happens. One of the things that happens is that the living can enhance God's general evaluation of the dead, while the dead can intercede for the living by providing God with their actual experience from which God can offer new possibilities to the living.

In this approach, is there anything like an interim state? It does not seem so. As explained here, the transition through death from this life to the afterlife is immediate. When a person's becoming ceases, God at once experiences that person fully. This is the basis for understanding immortality, resurrection, and judgment. There is a sense in which the afterlife as conceived here, continues to be related to the still-developing world of the living. Within that dynamic relationship, the dead are given back to themselves in a continual way by the experience of the living, and the relative contribution of the dead to the living does shift from one occasion to another. But this is not really an interim state. It is rather the permanent state of reality as interpreted relationally. There is not some other kind of state of existence still to come that makes this situation an interim one. This aspect of the total view will be discussed in the next chapter on eschatology.

Likewise, this view does not envision a condition like hell as it is typically understood. A thoroughly relational view is all-inclusive, at least in reference to God. *We* may and do exclude from our experience certain things or people. In fact, we probably exclude most of what is realistically available to us. This act of exclusion is another way of saying we are limited; we simply cannot experience everything, nor do we experience what we do in a complete way.

This leads to a relational view of freedom. As was stated above, the possibility of hell seems to be required by our understanding of freedom. The understanding assumes that freedom is a choice between mutually exclusive alternatives. A relational view does not see freedom this way because it does not see things as mutually exclusive but mutually connected. Our freedom means we choose what we experience and to the degree we decide. But every choice is a renewal of relationship with the whole, with God. We don't have the freedom to eliminate all relationship because freedom is for relationship.

So God's judgment is not inclusive of some and exclusive of others. God's judgment is a graded or ranked evaluation of everything and everyone. The ranking means that there is a spectrum of most to least valuable. The least valuable experiences or events or persons are those from which God can derive virtually nothing that will contribute to the future development of his relation to the world. What would such a minimal experience be? In the case of the brother who committed suicide, it might mean that his experience of life and of himself turned out to be so empty, so undesirable, so negative that very little can be gleaned from it to offer as a stimulus or as new possibilities for others.

On the other hand, his struggle to find meaning, the liberation he may have felt in finally *choosing* to end his life, the benefit he may have felt by removing himself as "troublesome" to others could actually be valuable experiences that God can use positively to stimulate more meaningful actiondecisions in the minister-brother, for example. In general, a person's life is valuable, a contribution to God to the degree the person's experiences include freedom, novelty, choice, decision, feeling. A person who tends to conform, be repetitious, obey, go along, repress has less value to contribute.

Obviously, these general characterizations must be nuanced with particular circumstances and qualifications, but the general orientation of value is between creativity, novelty, decision and repetition, sameness, conformity. The former way of life is more valuable because it generates more possibilities, a wider range of experience, greater versatility. The latter perpetuates what already is and weakens the thrust toward newness. Nonetheless, whatever one's life experience, it *is* a contribution to God and through God to the world. Nothing is excluded.

On the other side of this consideration, to anticipate being with God, while God goes about the divine activity of drawing new possibilities, is to anticipate a constantly changing, new, dynamic process to which we continually contribute ourselves. This is a far cry from a rather static contemplation of a perfect and changeless God. Further, if we live by such a vision in this life, it means we are seeking the most creative, novel, stimulating, intense experience in virtually everything we do. No situation is trivial or useless in this perspective because every situation is a contribution to God, more or less valuable depending on how we live it, what experience we actually make of it. Obviously, some situations have more potential than others. Every case we've looked at in this book has far more inherent value than going grocery shopping, taking a shower, reading the newspaper, or going to sleep. But even these ordinary events can be invested with as much feeling, meaning, self as they are capable of.

This approach clearly stresses the value of the present. In every moment the relational question is: What is the potential of this situation and how can that be experienced most fully? This question is not originally ours. It is our way of trying to get in touch with what God is offering us. God's offer is always complete, i.e., it includes all the possible answers and communicates them in the priority God sees. Thus, every situation is charged with the dynamism of God's relationship to us, which lays before us the challenge of our freedom and the possibility of making our contribution to God.

Heaven is not a completely new state of existence; it is a constantly new realization of the contribution our lifetime makes to God and through God to the world. For a truly theocentric faith, there can be no delight, no satisfaction, no awareness more desirable, more appealing, more exciting. And at that point we may ask: Why would we want it to end? Why would God want it to end? Does it end? These are questions for chapter six.

Practical Implication

The minister was disturbed by the sense of responsibility his brother's suicide aroused in him, and he was concerned about

God's judgment. The relational view presented here would certainly affirm our responsibility for one another, but that responsibility is not limited to our activity with others while both we and they are alive. In a relational approach, there is a continuing influence, mediated through God, between the living and the dead. Put another way, the minister's responsibility for his brother doesn't end at the brother's death. By his continuing relationship (through prayer, memory, example, story, etc.), he goes on contributing to God's evaluation of his brother by adding new, actual experiences that affirm the brother's value. These contributions are, of course, put in relation to everything else, so it is not a question of our trying to tell God something God does not already know, or persuading God to change the evaluation of someone, like the brother who commits suicide. God's evaluation is God's experience of what actually is, but what actually is keeps happening and we contribute to it. In this way, our continual, new contributions are an extension of our responsibility to others.

This view should not undercut our responsibility to others while they are alive. The minister's contribution to his brother after the suicide is severely reduced in comparison to the contribution he could have made before the suicide. The reason for this is that before the suicide the brother was still an active, relating, becoming person. He had a range of choices before him and his action-decisions were still to be determined. None of this is true after death. The brother has become who he is; the possibilities for his further actual development are ended. The value of his actual life might increase as other events occur and are added to the accumulation of the whole. But that is a slight advance when compared to the possibilities during life. So, the extension of responsibility beyond death and the contribution we can make in this way is not equivalent to what we can and should do before death; there is no safety valve here to catch up or make up for our irresponsibility during a person's lifetime. Opportunities missed are missed; new opportunities are relative to actual conditions. After death, there are still opportunities to contribute to another person, but those opportunities are severely limited to the actual condition of the one who has died. In a relational view, the present is always of paramount importance.

A second practical implication of this view is that it can relax anxiety about God's judgment of us. If everything and everyone is included in God, then there is no reason to fear condemnation in the classic sense of exclusion from God. Even if we think we are capable of choosing against God, God accepts that very choice and draws from it something new. We cannot annihilate our relationality; we simply do not have that power. Despite our most deliberate acts of opposition, we cannot move outside of God's relationship to us. Our freedom is not a power to choose between absolutely exclusive alternatives; it is a power to choose among related options. We can choose more or less freely, more or less valuably, but we cannot opt out absolutely. God won't let us do that because God sees in every experience some possibility for contribution to the future. And God's vision/experience of itself draws us back into relationship with God.

Thus, in a relational view, freedom is more limited than in another view, i.e., our freedom does not extend to the possibility of acting in a way that absolutely contradicts the nature and purpose of freedom. As pointed out above, this does not mean that all free choices are equally valued. Just the opposite is the case. No two choices are ever exactly equal. Each one is new and generates new possibilities. It is true, however, that every free actiondecision is more or less valuable relative to God's prior valuation of possibilities and God's subsequent evaluation of actuality. A continuum of degrees is thus produced that *is* the actual world and that is God's judgment. Everything is included in its proper place, i.e., where it actually belongs relative to everything else. Only God can see what that order is, which is why all judgment is ultimately God's.

· 6 ·

A Nation's Oppressive Death
The Question of the End of the World

Experience

The speaker had just finished a lecture on the Christian meaning of death. She was a theology student in a nearby seminary and worked in this parish for her field placement. She had agreed to give a series of talks during Lent on the theology of suffering and death. In this particular presentation she described the stages a person typically goes through when anticipating death. She related these to a growing, honest affirmation of belief in Jesus and acceptance of the power of his resurrection. She had prepared well and prayed over her material so that it would be sincere and personal. She felt good about her presentation as she ended. A question period followed.

At first, no one asked any questions. It seemed like everyone was caught up in the faith-witness and openness of this obviously Christian woman. Then someone raised his hand. He was a refugee who had recently come to the U.S. and who had been attending the parish church for about a month. Although he was unfamiliar with many American customs, he handled English quite will. He began to speak carefully and calmly.

He thanked the speaker for her beautiful and encouraging talk.

It was clear to him that she believed what she had spoken, but he wanted to make one observation. In his experience, most of the people in the world do not die as she had described, thinking through the meaning of their death in relation to a reasonably good life they had enjoyed and don't want to let go of. Most people die because they starve or have no medical help or are killed in war or simply cannot escape persecution, oppression, neglect, or abuse. He just wanted everyone to remember how these people die and how many of them there are.

The man knew what he was talking about. He had been raised in extreme poverty. He was one of six children, only three of whom survived infancy. His father died at the age of forty; his mother had been living with his sister for the last ten years. She had worked in the fields all her life to provide what she could for her children. Now she too was in poor health, although she had not reached fifty. She had done everthing possible to give her children a good education because she believed that might help them escape the life they had been born into.

The man who had spoken at the parish meeting was the most successful in taking advantage of his mother's efforts. He had done well enough in school to qualify for a scholarship to college, where he excelled. From there, he won another scholarship to study in Europe and earned a doctorate in economics. His goal throughout was to return to his native land, try to give his mother and family a better life, and educate his own people in economics and how they might improve their own security. He held a teaching position at a state university and had begun to realize his goals. He also married and started his own family. Then a new government came into power.

The new regime was much more restrictive and extremely suspicious. One of its targets was the university system. Anyone teaching in a way considered dangerous or subversive to the government was removed and either imprisoned or exiled. This economics professor got word that he was being investigated. His encouragement of economic reform and suggestions for reorganizing labor and the use of profits was considered very dangerous. He had never thought of himself as undermining his government or being anything but a patriot, but it was obvious that someone else was defining the terms. The risk was increasing daily.

Anticipating his fate, he had arranged for his wife and their infant son to leave the country, ostensibly to visit relatives on a holiday. His plan was more secretive. He was going to escape with several others who were hoping to get to the United States and be admitted as refugees. He felt he might be able to locate there for a time, maybe even permanently, and be reunited with his family.

After a perilous escape and difficult crossing, he and his friends managed to get to the U.S. His case was taken over by a church social-welfare agency, and one of the local congregations began sponsoring him. He was living temporarily with one of the families in the congregation. They had helped him obtain a job as a waiter in a restaurant that served his native food. Working nights, he was able to use mornings and his day off in the library, reading journals and trying to keep abreast of his field. The agency was trying to arrange for his family to enter the U.S.

All the help he had received was not able to offset his deep feeling of loneliness and alienation. He also had to cope (again) with the sharp contrast between the poverty and repression in his own country and the affluence and freedom in the U.S. It made him realize the disparities that fill the world. He was not exactly bitter or angry. He just felt victimized and wondered whether there was a justice he could rely on, whether the abuses he and his family and country had suffered would ever be righted.

Generally, he had kept these feelings to himself. Until tonight. As he heard the speaker describe the anxiety and resistance of basically affluent people facing death after a comfortable life, he could think only of the many people he knew, like his parents and relatives, who suffer so much so unjustly. In their name, if nothing else, he had to speak, not to refute what was being said but to put it in a larger context. His brief comment elicited some striking reactions.

A few people responded rather defensively, saying that they knew others are oppressed, but that they didn't feel responsible for that. They didn't think of themselves as oppressing the rest of the world. They worked hard and did the best they could, right at home. Some of them let it be known *they* had never been to Europe. They barely even got a two-week vacation each year.

Others said they didn't feel guilty either, but they did admit there is some responsibility to do what they could to help those who are oppressed. The problem often is knowing what to do. On a global scale, the issues were so many and so complex. That's why many of the parishioners liked the idea of sponsoring one person whom they could get to know and help. That may not be much but it is something. Many people agreed with this.

But one person stated honestly that when the idea of sponsorship was first proposed, it wasn't too appealing. It felt like one more request on an overcroweded agenda. The parish was already active in several social projects, not to mention the involvements of individuals on their own. There was only so much one person or one parish could take on.

Time for discussion was drawing to a close. The speaker politely thanked everyone and acknowledged that there had certainly been a lively discussion. Privately, she realized she had been thinking of death too narrowly and had not even considered the questions implied in the refugee's comment. Why do so many people live and die in oppressed conditions? What can we do about it? Does our theology have anything to say about this?

Theological Question

Lying behind the discussion after the speaker's lecture on death is the question of social responsibility. This question is posed by the fact of social injustice, oppression, and violence. What can we do? What does our Christian faith expect us to do?

The three basic reactions in the discussion typify the feelings of Christians toward these questions. There are some who feel no responsibility. This doesn't necessarily mean they are indifferent or calloused toward those who suffer. But mere awareness of social injustice does not bring with it any felt urgency to act to change the conditions that produce injustice. Unless we are directly responsible, many of us don't feel responsible at all. The question is: Are we responsible for the suffering of others in the world?

Even those who do feel some responsibility and want to do something about injustice don't always know what to do or how to do it. This is especially true if the problem is focused in another part of the world, but it can be in this country, or city, or community and the same question arises. Sometimes the question is just a way of avoiding responsibility, but most of the time it is a genuine concern. It is especially pressing if established channels for effecting change, like the legislative and judicial process, have been used and yielded meager or no results. Compared to the scope of the problem, small victories sometimes intensify the frustration and almost taunt continuing efforts. So the question is: What to do?

When *something* is done, it leads to other related problems and demands. Very quickly, those who accept and act on a social responsibility feel responsible for other problems and want to address them. As a result, they can be overwhelmed in no time with the relentless demands of social justice on their resources. In any event, to respond adequately to any social issue requires a person to be informed, to consider alternatives, to work with others, and to refrain from imposing judgments/stereotypes on those presumed to be the oppressors. In short, to respond to social injustice is a demanding and tiring and often futile task. And so the question arises: Why bother?

These three questions are tied together and related theologically to the question about God's response to social injustice and oppression and violence. God's response is God's judgment, and that has to do with the future. The future as the realm of God's judgment may be understood in two senses. One is a historical sense; the other is a final sense. In the historical sense, the future is the time still to come and what may happen in it. God's judgment is indeed an evaluation of the past, but it is also a projection of the future, a vision of what could be and from God's point of view what should be (if the future is to be all God sees it can be and wants it to be). In the final sense, the future is the end of time. It is the decisive event in which God's judgment on the whole of history is rendered with the corresponding outcome, customarily described as reward and punishment.

The hope that theology articulates is that the historical future really will contain a change from our present and past experience of injustice. It is an energizing impulse to work for *that* future and not to grow weary or abandon it altogether. The hope that theology articulates is also that the final future will at last redress the injustices that have been perpetrated throughout history. Even if the wrongdoers are not punished, the innocent sufferers will at least be rewarded. But prior to that, hope in the historical future is stressed because that is the realm where *we* can still do what God expects.

The task then for theology is to respond to the questions: Are we responsible? What do we do? Why bother? Theology's response comes from dwelling on God's response to social injustice. This means exploring the meaning of the twofold future and the hope it generates. Is hope in the historical future sufficient to preclude a final future of punishment for social injustice?

Theological Reflection

A typical theology of the future embraces two broad approaches. Each one relates differently to our social responsibility and identifies the object or goal of hope differently. One theological understanding of the future is "the last things." These are not really things, of course, but events. They are the final, definitive events in the life of an individual or of the whole world. Up to now our attention has been focused on the last things in the lives of individuals: personal death, particular judgment, immortality, an interim state, heaven/hell, and bodily resurrection.

When the last things refer to the life of the world or history as a whole, they customarily include the second coming of Jesus, the resurrection of the dead, general judgment (eliminating an interim state and resulting in heaven or hell), and the consummation of the world. The same parallel observed in previous chapters between philosophical and biblical sources appears here also. It is the parallel between individual and social, private and public, specific and general concerns. In terms of this chapter, the interest is in the end of the world. On this point a typical theology of the last things is extremely speculative. Speculation is inevitable, as has been pointed out above, for any reflection on death. But at least in the case of personal death, we have observed people dying and we can anticipate our own death by certain vicarious experiences (like sleep, trance, ecstasy, etc.). This isn't true for the end of the world. Individual existences end; the world does not, at least not in our experience of it.

At the same time, the biblical imagery associated with the end of the world is not very helpful. It strikes many people as fanciful and not very likely to be the way things will end (as was already noted in chapter five regarding the general resurrection). Even if this imagery is explained as a description suited to its own times, there isn't anything comparable to put in its place. And to the degree people do accept it as a revealed account of how the world will end, it tends to draw attention to the details of these events (feeding curiosity and missing the deeper meaning).

The result of an emphasis on the last things is that social responsibility is easily avoided or put off to the absolute end. This corresponds to the attitude of those who responded to the refugee by saying they felt no responsibility for social injustice because they were not directly oppressing others. We have a tendency to leap over everything between us and the last things. The time question that arises is, when will it occur, instead of, what can we do until then to improve the world and prepare for the last things? And when preparation for the last things is addressed, it is usually in terms of personal preparation for individual salvation. The last things provide the public context in which hope for personal salvation is located.

Even the biblical account of the last judgment can be used to feed into this preoccupation with personal salvation. The decisive issue appears to be how each individual deals with other individuals who are in need, not why there are still individuals in need at the end time. The hope associated with the last things is not primarily a social hope but a private hope that is guaranteed by personal action in a setting that is somewhat social. The deeper, original social dimensions of the biblical view are eclipsed when the last things are interpreted in such a highly individualistic way.

A second theological understanding of the future tries to be more integrally social. In this approach, the future is used to interpret the present. The future is not concentrated at the end, as with the last things, waiting to happen. Rather, the future is active; it exerts a genuine influence on the present. The future that does this is the future God has allowed us to glimpse in the divine activity in our previous history. Those events in which God gives us this glimpse form the core of salvation history from its origins down to the present day.

Thus, the future as interpretation is a collective vision, drawn from certain privileged experiences in the past. This vision is not just a memory of what has been. It is a view of what can be. This view is realistic (rather than utopian or illusory) because it is based on what actually has happened, but the future viewed in this way is not intended to be a repetition of what has happened. It is that privileged past projected beyond the particular factors and limitations of the past. Because the future does not have such limitations, it frees the experience of the past to become a new vision for the present. In this sense, the future interprets the present; it sketches the favored possibilities that the present can enact.

There are important implications in this view for social responsibility. The past events that are favored or privileged glimpses into God's vision of the future are usually events of liberation from various forms of oppression, injustice, violence. These events give rise to a future permeated by God's social concern and social commitment. That awareness alone underscores the value and necessity of social engagement, thereby reinforcing those who feel *some* social responsibility.

In addition, the vision of God projected into the future may also shed light on what can or should be done to alleviate current social problems. Both of these aspects were expressed by the second group of parishioners who responded to the refugee; they felt their social responsibility (and maybe needed that feeling reinforced) but didn't know what to do. The future as interpretation of the present aims at addressing both concerns.

But there are difficulties with this approach. The concrete meaning of "future" in this case is hard to specify, at least in a way that can be translated into social programs and action. It all remains fairly nebulous and perhaps not very useable practically. Partly for this reason a second difficulty arises. The specific content of the future that interprets the present is drawn from events of the past (whether the recent or the remote past). But *these* events must be interpreted too; indeed, a decision must be made about which *are* the privileged events. The glimpse of God's activity in these past events is just that, a glimpse. It needs elaboration, and the elaboration is prey to some infiltration of our own biases and preferences. This often means that our contentment with the status quo (especially if we benefit from it) takes over and interprets the future in such a way that it will confirm the present. Sometimes, too, it happens that people try to do all at once everything that the future holds out . This can give rise to the attitude described by some as being saturated, overworked, burned out. So even if the general account of this understanding of the future is accurate, it is very difficult to make that account more specific and to keep our own prejudices out when doing so.

How would a relational approach view our social responsibility and what sort of theological understanding of the future does it provide? In a thoroughly relational view, everything is related to everything else, and these relations are established through actual experiences or events. These two aspects contain important implications for social responsibility that may be stated as: There are no purely private acts, and nothing is determined until it is determined. The first point underlines our inescapable social responsibility; the second point emphasizes our power of freedom.

To say there are no purely private acts may seem to contradict our own experience. There are many things we do or think or feel that no one else knows about. And to some degree we can keep such things secret or withhold any public expression of them. Everything we do, however, is actual and has some effect outside of ourselves. In chapters one and two this was explained in terms of God's fully experiencing our experience and drawing from it *all* the possibilities for continued experience that each event generates. These possibilities are then offered to us by God as the continuum from which we create our next experience. This is already a public carry-over of our every private act. God's involvement guarantees that nothing remains entirely enclosed within our own world of experience.

The way this activity of God is communicated and experienced in the public realm will vary quite a bit. In general, what happens is that everything that actually constitutes a person's experience generates an influence that may be compared to a field or environment. We can often feel or sense this about another person without knowing very much specifically. We speak of "picking up the vibes," or gauging "the climate" of a meeting or encounter, or sensing "the mood" of a group, etc. All these expressions reflect the fact that something is being generated by and among people.

That something is not necessarily an intentional sharing of a person's ideas or feelings or experiences. For example, after the speaker finished her lecture, there was a certain mood in the group. That mood was the result of all the feelings and reactions and thoughts that the lecture had generated in the people present. Their reactions may have been private, but they were not purely private.

Likewise, when the refugee spoke, there were responses, even though at first they were not verbalized or clearly expressed in any other way. The spoken reactions sharpened and perhaps intensified the mood of the group, but the mood was already there before the words were spoken. And that is the point. Whatever we feel, it inevitably extends beyond our innermost selves no matter how hard we try to keep it suppressed. This does not mean that our private acts are always clearly and fully perceived by others. In fact, quite the opposite is the case.

It requires a good bit of attention usually to pick up, to sense, to enter into the environment generated by others. This is due to many factors. Sometimes we're more attentive to our own feelings and just aren't open to what others are generating. Sometimes we expect one kind of feeling (because of previous experience or biases or preconditioning) and don't sense what is really there. Sometimes the others *are* repressing or faking or distorting their private experiences. They may do this for all kinds of reasons, in all kinds of ways, and with all degrees of success. So we may not perceive accurately the environment that others' private experiences generate, but those experiences do generate an environment and it does influence us in one way or another. This is because everything is related to everything else in a relational view.

From this point of view, our social responsibility is inescapable. Everything we experience inevitably contributes to a social environment, i.e., to our feeling about the larger world we inhabit. And this feeling-for the larger world is the indispensable foundation for any eventual social action. This point overlaps with the explanation of original and social sin in chapter two. Negative, defensive, resistant feelings, like those expressed by some of the parishioners, contribute in that way to the environment that we inhabit and live in together. Even if those feelings are not expressed in some obvious, overt way, they are *there* and their influence is *felt*, and that is what social responsibility is about at its most primal level.

The other side of this, of course, is the environment generated by feelings of concern, compassion, justice, involvement, change, etc., like those expressed by some of the other parishioners. These feelings have their influence too, whether expressed explicitly or not. In fact, these feelings have an intrinsically greater influence because they are more like the feelings of God disclosed in the privileged events that give us a glimpse into God's future. Thus, they have a higher valuation in God's scheme of things and allow God to draw out more of the best possibilities for future enactment.

But because all of this is at a rather nebulous level of experience, it seems to many people to be either wishful, romantic thinking or weak by comparison with the tough, pragmatic, hard-nosed realism of action. There is a point here. To concentrate exclusively on being in touch with the mood or climate or feeling-for the world in any given situation is not yet *relating* to that world in a full, actual sense. This is where the power of freedom enters in.

The most free acts and the most powerful are those that actualize the aim which God offers as the best in any situation. How do we know what the best aim is? Ordinarily, it requires some real attending to the mood or climate of the situation. The feelings generated by the immediate, just-now-completed events are the best indicator of what God sees as the next best possibility. This may seem to undercut the value of objective norms and principles for right conduct. It is not intended to do that.

Stated principles and norms, what we call objective truth or morality, are an expression of the very feelings described above. These are privileged articulations, on a general level, of what we may expect to be in touch with concretely when we are in an actual, "live" situation. Put the other way around, our discernment of God's view *in the concrete* is experienced as feeling-for God's aim in the midst of all the variable factors and messages and possibilities in the same concrete situation. It is not a question of clear, objective norms *versus* ambiguous, experiential feeling, but rather a question of the interplay between the two. Both are allies working for the sake of the best, as God sees it, in every case. Together they can shape actiondecisions that more closely approximate God's vision.

This is power—the power to enter a situation openly, assuming as little as possible in this actual circumstance but grasping, sensing, feeling-for what God offers as the best possibility. This is free because it is not predetermined; it is powerful because it leads to actiondecisions that define this experience and thereby generate new possibilities for the future. These possibilities are more or less what they could be in God's view, depending on our actual decisions. Thus, we have power regarding the future; we decide what kind of environment we shall fashion and move into.

The ultimate failure of social responsibility is not to believe in our power and not to act on our freedom. That disbelief is made easier when we don't attend very carefully or regularly to the environment being generated all around us. Admittedly, this presentation gives us no concrete suggestions for how to discern more accurately God's vision, or how to spell out more strategically the steps to be taken to enact that vision. These are indispensable follow-on moments. The point of the discussion here is that a relational view affirms and explains both our social responsibility and the power we have to choose freely how we shall shape the social environment that we inhabit. There are no purely private acts, and nothing is determined until it is determined. How we determine/actualize the possibilities that our social responsibility generates depends in part on how we view the future.

In a relational approach, our understanding of the future as "the last things" is virtually impossible. This is because of the essential conviction that whatever is actual is in relationship, and relationship is understood as event, occurrence, making definite what is possible. So it is a contradiction in terms for a relational world to cease being in relation, i.e., to cease becoming altogether. This does not rule out the possibility, however, that the type of relationships we now experience could reach the level of a new *type* of relationship. What that may be we cannot say. What we can say is that any such development would have to be a true development, an outgrowth that is in real continuity with the nature of relating as we now experience it. Otherwise, we would be talking about a new kind of reality that relational categories would be inappropriate or inadequate to explain.

From a consistently relational point of view, even if there are radical developments and variations, there is no absolute end, no last things in the sense of a complete halt to relational experience. There is rather an indefinite continuing of the relational world that has been described up to this point. This leads to a very open-ended notion of the future. In fact, the only end point would seem to be our concept of the future itself. That is, we are bounded by or are heading toward that future which our experience of the past enables us to foresee. This is very compatible with the second theological understanding of the future described above.

One of the things a relational view would stress about the future seen in this way is that it is determined by the interaction of many forces. The future of just a single event is all the possibilities that event generates. These are perceived differently by all those in touch with that event and therefore enacted differently. The variety of perceptions and enactments means that the future of this one event is never a single, controlling, exclusive possibility. When this fact is extended to all the events that comprise our actual existence until now, the complexity of the future is staggering. To be sure, most of us tend to identify one or two strands of experience that we use to envision our future and enact our present. But if we take into account the total picture, it leads to a proliferation of possible futures, all of which coexist both in vision and in action.

This reinforces the importance of our freedom and the decisiveness of our choices. We are free to see what the future can be and therefore what the present can contribute to it. Our vision is not entirely left up to our own imagination. It is conditioned by the actual past, and that includes God's part in the past. All the possible futures are included in God's perfect knowledge of the past, but not all possible futures are equally desirable or valuable. God will not, however, force the divine vision on us or force us to enact it. Our freedom is real and God's commitment to relationship consistent.

What this all means is that relational theology orients us to review again and again God's vision of the future, to become so familiar with is that it hones our instincts and sensitivities and feelings for what God sees as our best future. That future is not our only option, but it is our best option. It opens our eyes to what can be done in the present and where those decisions will lead. It puts into our hands once more the power to determime how extensive or how narrow, how inclusive or how exclusive, how free or how limited the future is.

In order to stay in touch with the privileged expressions of God's view of the future, Christians return to the life of Jesus. Given the particular focus of this book, that means looking in a relational way at the death of Jesus and trying to see in that event the future that God prizes most of all. This will be done in the next chapter. If that vision can be made clear, then the possibility for enacting that future may be more attractive and the ultimate meaning of death may be seen.

Practical Implication

The observations of the refugee after the speaker's talk brought home the reality of our social responsibility. The reactions of the parishioners highlighted three further questions: Are we responsible? What can we do? Why bother? The relational view presented here responds to those questions by showing the inherent social responsibility all our experiences carry with them and by urging that careful attention be given to cultivating our feeling-for the future that God envisions, given the actual events of the past. In such a view, the typical theology of the last things virtually disappears, and the future appears as an ongoing, open-ended perception of what *can* actually be.

There are two practical implications of this view that need to be addressed. If there are no last things, no definitive conclusion to the world-history process, what happens to the conviction that justice will finally be done at the end and that all wrongs will be righted? Doesn't an open-ended view also increase the sense of futility in trying to change things for the better? Our efforts seem so ineffective, so incapable of reversing the magnitude of social suffering in the world. Both questions are serious challenges to the relational view described here.

There is no doubt that the prospect of a final day of reckoning has sustained many persons in the midst of unjust suffering and persecution. The sustenance has come from the belief that ultimately there is a God in control who will vindicate the innocent and requite the guilty, who will redress the wrongs and punish wrongdoers, who will restore justice and wipe away every tear. Is all of this discarded? Not really.

The significant difference in a relational view is that God alone is not ultimately in control. God-with-us, God-in-relation to us is ultimately in control. God can do only what can be done with us. God will not do what we will not do with God. God simply doesn't act unilaterally in a relational world. At the same time, God cannot be overcome by any contrary force because God draws whatever good there is from every situation. This is the relational understanding of what it means that God is "in control." God's control is not to impose or dictate or usurp or destroy. God's control is to keep relationships happening and to keep offering the best possibility for every relationship. The control is persuasive, luring, suggestive, visionary, creative.

Where does that leave the innocent victims of injustice? It leaves them, by virture of their innocent suffering, closer to the heart of God's deepest relationship to the world. This will be explained in the next chapter in connection with Jesus' death. The same point is affirmed in Scripture regarding the privileged position of the poor, and it has been reaffirmed forcefully in recent liberation theology. This claim for the privileged status of the poor is sometimes connected with the vindication at the end of the world as customarily understood.

The same privileged status of the oppressed can be explained relationally apart from the end of the world, in terms of the congruence of their experience and God's. The degree of congruence between their experience and God's means, in a relational view, that God draws the best possibilities for the future from their experience more than from the experience of others. And in light of the previous discussions of immortality, resurrection, and judgment, their sense of being for the world with God may be greater than that of most of us. In a way, this could be interpreted as a kind of vindication or reward at the end of *their* lives, even if it is not the end of the world as such. If taken this way, their reward does not mean a separation from the world but a more God-like relation to the world. And that is the ultimate reward that God can and wants to give in a relational perspective.

This brief discussion touches on the relational response to the other question about the success or futility of efforts to change the world. It is understandable that we measure our efforts in terms of discernible success. But in a relational view, this is a secondary criterion. The primary criterion is the intrinsic quality of one's experience in trying to improve the world. This means the degree of unity with God's priorities in every situation, whether or not the outcome is "successful" in terms of limited, specific results. Being-with God and freely feeling the future as God does is never futile or unsuccessful.

This is another instance of trying to maintain the correct priority. God is primary. Our identification with God's relationship to the world is primary. All else is secondary—not insignificant nor worthless nor negligible. As secondary, all else flows from and is enacted in order to make complete God's vision of the future. No enactment is futile if it flows in this way from an actual union with God. And that is why we should bother.

·7·

The Death of Jesus
Theological Test Case

Experience

The situations described in the previous six chapters represent typical experiences of death. They provoke a variety of questions that we want to respond to from the experience of our Christian faith as mediated by theology. In the first scenario, the grandmother's death, the dominant question is one of meaning. This question is asked at three levels: the meaning of death for God, for those who survive, and for the person who dies.

The second example shifts from a relatively controlled, reflective experience of death to a traumatic, shocking experience— the accidental death of a small child. Experiences of this type raise a different sort of question: Why? Behind that question is a feeling that some injustice is being worked or that God, who should prevent such things, no longer cares or is punishing the victims. At best, such experiences remind us graphically and painfully that we don't understand God well enough yet.

Even in such circumstances, Christians have usually taken consolation in the expectation of immortality. This appears in the third case of the husband who feels his wife's presence to be real in a new way. This raises the question of personal immortality: Is it real? What is it like for the person who dies? What connection, if any, is there between the immortal life of the dead and the mortal life of the living?

These questions are extended with consideration of our bodiliness and its ultimate value in God's view. This concern figures prominently in the case of cremation, which is disturbing to the sister who interprets that act as a violation of her sister and a threat to her resurrection.

Closely aligned with our interpretation of death, immortality, and resurrection is judgment. This is especially acute when a person appears to have lived a morally evil life or to have committed suicide, as in the instance of the minister's brother. Our anxious concern about how God judges our life is heightened in such circumstances because our responsibility for one another is more evident. Hence, judgment contains some additional questions: How will God judge us? When does judgment occur, immediately after death or at the end of the world or both? What are the ultimate, possible outcomes?

This level of questioning often remains centered on individuals and can overlook our social responsibility, indeed the interdependence of our individual lives with others. The social dimension is especially evident when we are reminded of how and why most people in the world die, a point made by the refugee in chapter six. This fact raises the question of the future as a time for final retribution, requiting of evil, and dispensing of rewards and punishments.

A general theology of death can be framed to respond to these questions, and that has been done here by combining a typical theology with a more relational one. The result is a theology that tries to be an appropriate expression of our belief and an adequate explanation of our actual experience of death. For any theology of death, the crucial test case is the death of Jesus. This is the central event around which the origins of Christianity pivot. By interpreting his death as both the revelation and empowerment of new life in God's Spirit, Christians claim that God's promises are fulfilled and our destiny made possible. Seen in this way, Jesus' death is not taken in isolation from his earthly life or his resurrection. It is rather a focal point for viewing his life as a whole and for interpreting its meaning fully.

That meaning is typically supported by interconnected claims. One is that Jesus' death is a *unique* event in human history. It is in a class by itself, a once-for-all event. Nothing like it had ever happened before and nothing like it can ever happen again. It should be remembered that Jesus' death has this character because the same is true for his whole life. The uniqueness of his life culminates in his death, while his death is the culmination of his life. In other words, *Jesus* is unique, and his death is a special instance of this claim.

A second claim is that Jesus' death has *universal* effect. This is part of its uniqueness. Although the actual event occurred in one place, at one time, and was limited by all the conditions of a historical setting, Jesus' death is understood to be beneficial for all people, in all places, at all times. Jesus' death focuses in a special way the paradoxical tension between the local and the universal, the individual and the many, the past and the present, which characterizes the Jewish and Christian experience of God in our lives.

The effect that Jesus' death has is salvific. Salvation is usually understood as the fulfillment of persons, the realizing of all we can be, although sometimes salvation is presented in minimal terms. This occurs when we think of heaven as the place of salvation and when we ask what must we do to "get in," or when we think of heaven or salvation as requiring a way of life on earth that really limits our happiness or natural desires or human goals. So in an attempt to have the best of both, we can fall into the mindset of "how much can I get away with and still be saved?"

Clearly, this is not the outcome that our theological explanation of salvation desires. In its best expression, salvation has been understood as the fulfillment of our humanness, of our best selves, and not as inhibiting our human potential. This is made clear with regard to our capacity for freedom. Salvation, which is what we were made for, is freely offered and elicits a free response. No one is forced to be saved (by God anyway, even if some church persons exert pressure), and no one is saved automatically. Through Jesus, a real, attainable possibility has been inserted into the horizon of human becoming, but it must be appropriated by us.

God certainly wants all people to be saved, and in Jesus God has done everything divinely possible to see to it that all people are saved. But one thing God won't do is take away our freedom. This leads to two specific questions: How is God's desire that all people be saved actually worked out, and what role does Jesus' death play in that working out? The second question is also sometimes asked in terms of how explicitly or consciously one must identify with Jesus in order to be saved. These further questions result from the prior claim that Jesus' death has a universal effect.

The third claim undergirds the previous two. Jesus' death is understood to be a unique event and have universal effect because of Jesus' *divinity*. Who Jesus ultimately *is* clarifies what Jesus actually *did* and what value that action has. To understand Jesus' divinity is a constant challenge for Christian theology. In one sense, the persuasiveness of the claims made for Jesus' death stands or falls with the adequacy of theology's explanation of Jesus' divinity. At the same time, these claims and the original experiences that generated them are a source of insight into who Jesus is. So the theological task must be met holistically, by relating experience and interpretation continually and reciprocally.

A relational approach should be in a good position to do this. The rest of this chapter will present the potential of a relational view for explaining Jesus' death—the crucial test case. This explanation clusters around the three claims just discussed: uniqueness, universality, and divinity. The implications of a relational interpretation for the dominant questions raised in the cases will be discussed briefly at the conclusion.

A Relational Christology

On the surface it appears that a relational view is unable to affirm the three theological claims made for Jesus' death. Regarding uniqueness, a relational approach affirms different *degrees* rather than different *kinds* of experience or event. This is evident in the basic view of God's relationship to us. God is the perfection or fullness of what actually is, but God is not understood as an exception or radically other kind of being. God's uniqueness is explained in terms of God's fullness, the most complete degree of actuality that is possible. If this is true for God, it is no less true for an event like Jesus' death.

The emphasis on degree of difference is also seen in a relational understanding of immortality, resurrection, judgment, heaven and hell. Everything that is actual participates in the same kind of existence, what might be called the essence or nature of actuality. There is a great range of degrees within the nature of actual existence; a relational approach affirms this range of degrees as adequate to explain reality as we experience it. That is consistent with its own principles, but is questionable as an adequate explanation of the uniqueness of Jesus' death as we have typically understood it.

In a similar way, the universal effect of Jesus' death seems to be undercut by the relational view that God includes all experiences and all events and all people in God's relation to the world. This means that nothing actual is ever really lost as far as God is concerned. If this is so, what does it mean to say that *Jesus'* death is the unique event that has universal effect? From another point of view, our customary approach assumes that there are mutually exclusive options. Our freedom is exercised in regard to these options. We choose either for God, salvation, Jesus or for ourselves, our existence, this world. Such absolute exclusiveness is not really conceivable in a relational view. Rather, there are degrees of choice. If we can't really choose not to relate to God, what universal effect does Jesus' death have? By our relational nature, we are already and always included in the realm of freedom where we can truly choose, but among options that are ultimately compatible, not exclusive.

Finally, both of the previous claims are grounded in Jesus' divine relation with God. As developed typically, this claim embraces equally the humanity and divinity of Jesus. What this means is often seen more sharply in the interpretations that have been rejected than in the positive formulations of orthodox dogma. Nonetheless, a thoroughly relational view poses two problems. It tends to be rigorously monotheistic. As presented in this book, relational theology deals with God and the world. Reflection on the nature of God apart from this relationship falls outside the scope that relational theology can address.

In addition to its monotheistic stress, this approach affirms God's relationship to everything and everyone that is actual. This would seem to suggest a degree of divinity in everything, or that everything has a divine character in God. Once again, it is a matter of degrees. But is that sufficient to explain the divinity of Jesus as it has been believed by Christians? Is such a superior-degree-of-divinity Christology not one of the false interpretations previously considered in Christian history and rejected?

These initial reservations are not, of course, the final word. But they must be addressed before turning to a more direct presentation of a relational view of Jesus' death. What makes anything unique? Is it in being an exception, strictly speaking, to everything else, or is it in being like everything else but more fully, more completely? In the latter case, uniqueness is also a model, an ideal, a possibility to aim at. We can see ourselves approximating what is like us. In the former case, uniqueness is eccentric, curious, distracting. We can't see ourselves wanting or needing to be like it.

Uniqueness as fulfillment and model is how Christians have viewed Jesus' life and death. He is the supreme model that is attainable because he lived our kind of life and died our kind of death. In him we can see ourselves. To the extent that he appears as a totally other kind of person, we lose connection with him. This has sometimes happened in the past when Jesus' divinity was stressed in a one-sided manner, making him seem like someone so unique, so unlike us that he ceased being a realistic model. In that respect, others took his place: Mary his mother, saints, church practices, etc.

Another way of expressing the uniqueness of Jesus' death is by analogy. Analogy is a comparison or relationship in which differences are viewed within a more fundamental sameness. The relational view put forth here is akin to analogy. Within the fundamental sameness of death, Jesus' death is unique because it expresses *everything* that a human death can really be. We may not be able to grasp all at once or simply what that is, but if we proclaim Jesus' death to be unique in this way, that is one of the implications.

Another implication brought out clearly in a relational view is that a uniquely complete event like Jesus' death is not static. It is not an isolated moment to be viewed and imitated. In a relational view, everything is related to everything else in an actual way, as mutually influencing and being influenced. The degree of *active* relating depends on the completeness of the events, experiences, persons experiencing. From our side, this means that Jesus' death enhances our own death when we are united to him. From Jesus' side, this means our death reenacts his to some degree and gives it a new, though never more complete, expression. Thus, the uniqueness of Jesus' death does not separate that event from us but brings it closer, drawing together still more intimately the union between Jesus and us. How this is explained in a relational way leads to the second claim for Jesus' death—its universality.

In a relational view, the key to universality is in the activity of God. It is God who draws from every occasion all the possibilities for continued experience, and it is God who offers us those possibilities in the order of what is best from God's point of view. In this way, any previous event can exert some influence on any subsequent event. Now, in a relational approach, activity acquires value insofar as it becomes something definite. While an event is happening, it is not yet clear what its value will be because it is not yet finalized. In this sense, it is only as things come to an end that they have a value that extends beyond their own experience of becoming.

To speak of Jesus' universality is to speak of a value that extends beyond Jesus himself. It is a value that God mediates to all, once Jesus has completed the event in his own experience. Regarding death, at least human death, Jesus' experience is the most complete experience that is possible. From this definite occasion, God can now derive new possibilities for everyone else who dies. The fact that Jesus' death is the fullest expression of what it is to die does not mean that people after Jesus die a lesser death than he did (experientially), but that they can die a fuller death than *they* would have otherwise. Other events in Jesus' life would have the same effect for the equivalent events in our life, like love, freedom, self-giving, etc. But all such events are part of the whole person's entire life. It is death that uniquely (in the sense of fullest) concretizes, makes final, and unifies our whole lifetime of such experiences.

Thus, the universality of Jesus' death is mediated by God to all people, but Jesus' death has the effect it does because it is a unique experience of what death for a human person can be. What *that* is will be spelled out shortly, but first a word about Jesus' divinity is in order. The basis, once again, is God and God's activity. In ordering or ranking the best possibilities for every new occasion, God's overriding value is creativity. Creativity implies a degree of newness, but it also implies a change or transformation in order to achieve newness. The divine principle that constantly seeks creative transformation in everything may be described as God's Logos —the divine, creative Word that expresses the very life of God.

The Logos is operative in everything God does, luring, drawing, beckoning the most creative (and therefore the most divine) experience possible out of the actual accumulation of experience up to this point. This framework suggests that the Logos of God has always existed with God and always seeks concrete expression in relation to the created world. As Christians, we believe that in Jesus the fullest possible expression of the Logos in human experience is manifested. From a consistently relational point of view, this is explained as the relationship between God's Logos and Jesus as the twin poles of one, actual existence. The same two poles or dynamic factors are operative in all of our lives, but not to the same complete degree as in the life of Jesus. Whether this difference of degree is because the Logos is uniquely related to Jesus from the beginning or because Jesus uniquely responds to the Logos throughout his lifetime is part of the mystery of the incarnation.

A typical theology would opt for the former position. Because the Logos is uniquely with Jesus at his very conception, Jesus is the divine one. A relational view could also assert this, but it would not consider the relationship *at* the beginning to be the exclusive emphasis. Rather, the relationship of the Logos to Jesus *from* the beginning was and continued to be the fullest unity possible throughout Jesus' lifetime. At any given moment (when he was twelve, when he was baptized, when he first began preaching, when he chose his disciples, etc.) the actual potential for the relation between the Logos and Jesus was different from any other given moment. This is simply what a relational view means. At *every* moment, however, the relationship of the Logos and Jesus was *all* that it could be. There was a perfect, full, complete congruence between the Logos of God and Jesus.

This complete congruence was as much Jesus' doing as it was the doing of the Logos. That is, Jesus had to respond to, had to actualize the best possibility that the Logos offered him. Jesus' unique response in every situation made possible new, creative opportunities that the Logos received from Jesus' actual actiondecisions and fed back into Jesus' life-possibilities. In this way, the real, dynamic relationship between the Logos and Jesus sustained a unique harmony or congruence that is called Jesus' divinity. Viewed from the side of the Logos, Jesus is the incarnation of the divine principle of creative transformation. Viewed from the side of Jesus, he became the Christ, one with the Logos of God, through a lifetime of congruent actiondecisions culminating in his death. Both views must be affirmed simultaneously to have an adequate understanding of Jesus' divinity.

A relational approach affirms the uniqueness, universality, and divinity of Jesus and of Jesus' death. It understands these claims consistently with its own principles and view of reality. This view is unmistakably different from that of typical theology. At one level, the difference may be seen as only one more indication of the pluralism that abounds in today's world. But at another level, the importance of that difference must be tested. For a different explanation that expresses the truth of Christian belief is one thing; a different explanation that distorts or misrepresents or falsifies the truth of Christian belief is another.

Ultimately, the criterion for deciding such an essential point is not logic and intellectual argument. It is whether a given explanation enables us *to live* the meaning of our belief. For Christianity is above all a way of life before it is a formulation of belief or a set of doctrines. What sort of meaning does a relational view of Jesus' death enable us to live? How is the meaning of Jesus' death to be understood? To answer these questions, it may be helpful to go back to the first chapter in which the general question of death's meaning was raised and to ask the same question of Jesus' death. What does Jesus' death mean for God, for Jesus himself, and for us?

A Relational Theology of Jesus' Death

The primary meaning of anyone's death in a relational view is the meaning for God. In general, everyone's death is a contribution to God in the sense that death finalizes each person's novel experience of life. As an actual, unrepeatable experience, this is something God desires and uses to foster continued advancement in the lives of others. Even though everyone's life and death is a contribution to God, the contributions are not equal. In fact, each person's contribution is relative to that person's possibilities in life (personal judgment) and relative to the actual accomplishment of others (general judgment).

What contribution does Jesus' death make to God? Typical theology asserts that this is the unique, decisive event that has effected salvation for all people. One of the familiar ways of saying this is that Jesus has reconciled us, as sinners, with God, who is holy. Various explanations of redemption or satisfaction have been developed to clarify what this reconciliation is and how it was accomplished. All such theories grapple with the fact of human sinfulness as the primary, disruptive element in the relationship between us and God.

A relational approach also asserts that Jesus' death is the unique, decisive event that effects salvation for all people. This is explained, however, not so much as restoring a relationship once established and subsequently broken, but as contributing a uniquely complete experience of the ideal relationship with God. From this experience, God is able to derive and offer to us uniquely complete opportunities for actualizing our own relationship with God. Thus, in a relational view, the ongoing, ever-new, interdependent quality of our relationship with God is given strong emphasis.

At the same time, Jesus' death has a once-for-all character and is understood as overcoming sin. The once-for-all aspect, the ultimate decisiveness of Jesus' death, means that this experience remains unsurpassable and always present as an operative part of God's relationship with us. It is from this unique event that God chooses new possibilities for *our* future. No other event gives God the same full range of experience to draw upon. That is part of its contribution to God. In addition, this view explains how Jesus' death overcomes sin and redeems us. The new possibilities that God derives for us from Jesus' death are offered to us in the midst of our *real* circumstances. These include sin. But sin is never able to obliterate the possibility of good, which God constantly offers us through Jesus. Without Jesus' death, God could draw upon only our own previous good acts to offer us new opportunities. Because our goodness is mingled with sin, the ultimate, decisive power of the possibilities we could generate for God would always be dubious. But Jesus' death, lived out in the midst of a sinful world, also settles the doubt once and for all.

In this way too, the universal effect of Jesus' death is seen through God's mediation. A person need not be consciously adhering to the memory of Jesus to benefit from Jesus' death. God derives possibilities for all people from the experience of Jesus. How effectively they may be communicated or how fully they may be enacted will depend on particular circumstances. At this point, being in conscious, explicit affiliation with Jesus may enhance the likelihood of a person's perceiving and following the best course of action, but it would not simply determine *whether* that person benefitted from Jesus' death.

Thus, the contribution of Jesus' death to God is that it gives God an actual, complete experience from which God can always draw new possibilities that, if we enact them, will enable us to overcome sin, fulfill our own destiny, and intensify the relationship between us and God. If this is the contribution of Jesus' death to God, what was there about *his* death that made this possible? What was his experience that gives God this unsurpassable source of opportunities?

To answer this question we need to take a closer look at any experience in a relational view. It was mentioned earlier that God's overriding aim in everything is creativity. This may also be expressed as the newest possible experience, given the reality out of which it emerges. A new experience, a creative experience, changes or transforms what is already there. In doing so, new feelings are generated. The newer, more creative the experience, the more intense the feelings. Such intensity is not a pressure or burden or neurotic emotion.

The most helpful analogy is aesthetics. Intensity of aesthetic experience is satisfying, uplifting, energizing. It excites and freshens and carries us beyond ourselves. We feel everything else a little differently after a good symphony or an engaging novel or a challenging play or a striking sculpture or a colorful painting. Our feeling for everything is intensified, enriched, deepened, made more sensitive and perhaps more sensory.

This intensity occurs when different elements are brought together in a new way. The bringing together requires some basis of compatibility. Within that compatible range, the goal is to find the most different elements. The history of art is, in one sense, the story of the effort to keep searching for new ways to bring together the most different elements imaginable. The same process underlies life itself. The fact is, however, that the immediate past has an extremely powerful influence on the immediate future. Most of us tend to repeat what we have once done. If it is familiar and if it seems effective, we stay with it (whatever "it" may be: where we sit at meetings, what kind of car we drive, where we go to eat, what we do to celebrate, etc.).

Now there are obvious advantages to routines or habit, especially for the more insignificant things we do (like shopping, hygiene, getting to work, etc.). In fact, habits can free our creative energy and imagination for more important things (like sustaining friendships, expanding personal interests, cultivating family, etc.). Here is the challenge: not to let our whole lives be channeled into routines, into expectations others have set up, into habits that limit our creativity. If God's overriding aim is creative transformation, that should be ours too. When we do act creatively, we give God more of what God wants, and that enables God to give back more to the world.

What has all this to do with Jesus' death? Jesus' death is an event that, like any other event, seeks the most creative experience possible. This is achieved when the greatest differences are brought together on a compatible basis. What differences does Jesus' death bring together? A relational view might describe these as the human capacity to receive and the divine capacity to give. The contrast lies in the fact that this exchange is carried to its fullest without the human capacity being absorbed into the divine or the divine capacity being wasted on the human.

The risk is higher on the human side. The sense that we might be engulfed by the divine, swallowed up in the transcendent, thereby losing our identity and very being, is an abiding feeling that remains part of our human experience and grounds our religious expression. At no point in our human experience is that possibility more acute than at death. In this event preeminently, we face the possibility of our extinction. To face that possibility in its fullness with the most complete openness and receptivity to God is to push the contrast to its limit. This is what happened in Jesus' death. Through it, Jesus gave God the experience of how far the human capacity can reach and still be human. By holding nothing back, Jesus allows God to feel what the human-divine relationship, contrasted in this way, stretched to its maximum, can be.

At the same time, God takes a risk. Offering the fullness of divine life is no guarantee it will be accepted. The gift could be refused. In a typical theology, this would not ultimately affect God because God is understood as perfect apart from any relationship to creation. But in a relational view, this is not so. God is interdependent with us and needs our experience to know *actually* what an ideal, complete relationship with us would be. So the death of Jesus has a definite contribution to make to God in terms of God's experience of the human capacity to receive as well as the divine capacity to be received, i.e., to have the gift that is offered actually received.

Such an experience is not simply the result of sin. Even if human beings had never sinned, there would still be the desire to extend the mutual capacities of us and God, to see how far they could go. In terms of God's relationship to us, this could even be understood as the ultimate aim in God's creative purpose. Once fulfilled, this experience becomes the norm according to which all human-divine relationships are evaluated and the ultimate source from which the new possibilities for the human-divine relationship are drawn.

This explanation does not radically alter the biblical affirmation that Jesus died for us, that he gave himself up on our behalf, that he carried out his Father's will. A relational view seeks only to express in relational terms how that proclamation may be understood. The interdependent, cocreative relationship between us and God reaches a unique, complete, full actualization in the death of Jesus. Because of this event, God now knows experientially how far the human capacity can reach. And God knows experientially how full the divine capacity is to give when the human capacity is at its maximum. This divine, experiential knowledge is manifested best in what Jesus' death means for Jesus.

Jesus' Death for Himself

If Jesus' death contributes to God a unique experience of the human capacity to receive God, then Jesus' death also allows God a unique opportunity to give. What does God give? The divine experience. There are two points to make here. One concerns how the experience is given; the other concerns what the experience is.

God gives to us by relating to us, and to relate is to enter in, to become part of, to feel together. These very human words are applicable to God in a relational view. God relates to us by feeling or experiencing what we feel, sharing new possibilities with us communicated as new feelings, impulses, attractions for our own enactment. Throughout, God is with us, indeed within, in the midst of our total life experience. God's presence is woven all through our experience. Our relationship with God is fashioned out of real, mutual, internal relations.

God's presence is not all we sense, and for some, God's presence may be one of the last things they sense. But for Jesus, God's presence was always primary. God's feelings became Jesus' feelings; God's vision became Jesus' vision; God's aim in all things became Jesus' aim. This perfect congruence is how a relational view understands Jesus' divinity, although saying it this way may suggest that Jesus only gradually became divine, whereas he was always human. A relational view would say that Jesus was always as fully divine as his humanness allowed. If humanity and divinity are really distinct (as typical theology expresses with two natures, human and divine), then these two distinct elements are related to each other. In a relational view, this means they are mutually related; they are interdependent; each conditions what the other is or can be at any given moment.

As Jesus developed humanly, his capacity for divinity developed as well. Whereas a gap opens up between these two poles for the rest of us, a perfect congruence or harmony characterized Jesus. His was always a perfectly actualized capacity for divine experience. And what was the divine experience? As noted before, the experience of creativity, or more pointedly in a human context, the experience of freedom. As Jesus experienced and acted on the divine freedom that coconstituted his own identity, he revealed certain characteristics that give us, who are at more of a distance from God than Jesus was, a glimpse into divine freedom.

God's freedom is paradoxical in the sense that it calls into question every previous expression of divine freedom that becomes settled, habitual, routinized. God's freedom remains free only by transcending itself, by going beyond its own actualization. A more relational way of saying this is that God's freedom must be reenacted to be free—not repeated slavishly, with full attention given to the particular details and circumstances, but reenacted, taken up anew in fresh acts of free, creative activity. This paradoxical thrust is evident in Jesus' intention to fulfill the Law by, at times, violating the specific precepts of the Law. It is not unfree repetition but free enactment that fulfills, and Jesus experienced this from God.

Divine freedom is threatening because nothing is immune from it. If God relates to everyone and everything and if God's way of relating is through free, creative transformation, then God's future remains essentially open. And so should ours. But we find it hard to live that way. We want to have assurance, foreknowledge, guarantees, and we don't want to feel that our previous efforts have all been for nought. So we tend to preserve and defend rather than push our capacity to receive God's next creative lead. In this respect, Jesus was clearly perceived as a threat by others. But he also must have felt himself and his ministry threatened by God's freedom. And yet, he responded with an ultimate openness and trust, even when he faced the seemingly contradictory outcome that God's freedom required Jesus' death. In fulfilling that last step, Jesus became forever the final threat to everything we claim in order to protect ourselves from God's freedom.

Jesus' experience of divine freedom is self-validating because there is nothing more from God to experience. If God's overriding aim in every occasion is creative transformation, freedom, then no relationship to God can experience anything more than that, although it is possible to experience less. Those who experience less often put the burden of proof on those who experience more. They want to be convinced on some other grounds that divine freedom is what it appears to be in the life of one who experiences it fully. Because they take their own partial experience as the norm, anything more seems to be blasphemy or a reckless disregard of tradition. But divine freedom has no other argument than itself when it is experienced, and if it is not experienced, no argument is adequate. Thus, God's freedom remains always an invitation to be accepted freely, not by the compulsion of argument or proof.

Finally, the experience of divine freedom is hopeful because it constantly pushes beyond the immediate, the given, the known to what else is possible. Divine freedom is never merely settled or permanent. It moves; it is active. To experience that and to make it the center of life, as Jesus did, is to be driven with urgency and filled with hope. It is to be discontent with the present as the sum total of all that can be. The experience of divine freedom means that we are constantly freed to stretch our dreams and hopes and efforts so they may be matched by God's creative response.

Jesus' death meant for Jesus that he experienced God's creative freedom not as something external to him, like an ideal or goal, but as the very innermost drive of his own life. There were many counterforces to that freedom, but he never replaced God's primacy with anything else. His lifetime of experiencing God's freedom culminated in his own final act of openness to what God could do with his death. And the story of *that* creative transformation has been told ever since.

Jesus' Death for Others

In the telling and retelling of Jesus' resurrection, the focus tends to shift toward its implications for us. This is certainly understandable and acceptable as long as the primary focus (God's creative transformation of Jesus' complete openness) is not obscured or subordinated. Jesus' death does have meaning "for us." A relational approach explains that meaning in terms of the field of influence that Jesus' death generates.

Jesus' death culminates a process of mutual, internal relatedness between Jesus and God that stretches the human capacity to receive and the divine capacity to give as fully as possible. This relationship actually occurred. It becomes part of the total accumulation of what actually is, not just what could be. As an actual occurrence, it is always available as a source from which God can derive new possibilities for others to experience and make actual in their own lives.

The relative effect of any new possibility depends on several factors. It depends first of all on the quality of the experience from which the possibility is derived. In the case of Jesus' death, that quality is the highest (most intense). The effect also depends on the nature of the experience. If it is a rare experience, which few people are likely to reenact, its effectiveness is lessened. We all die; Jesus' death has maximum relevance to human experience. The effect is also dependent on the compatibility of one experience with another. What Jesus and God experienced to the fullest is the basic structure of the relationship between God and all of us.

This basic, similar structure is the human capacity to receive divine experience and the divine capacity to give it, culminating in the final act of human openness to God—death. It would not be too far-fetched to imagine the actual fulfillment of this relationship between Jesus and God as a kind of magnetic field attracting our own still possible relationships with God. Such an attraction is not a controlling or usurping of our own free determination of how that relationship will actually turn out. It is, rather, a support, a contribution, a reinforcement of our own best possibilities and impulses in relation to God. Moreover, we can choose to enter more or less fully into the influence of this field. Specific action-decisions like prayer, intercession, memory of Jesus, funerals, preaching, Scripture accounts, devotions, etc., all have relative value in orienting us toward a fuller reenactment of Jesus' death in our own lives.

The underlying conviction in a relational view is that everything is related to everything else. An event as central and complete as the death of Jesus is not only related to everything else, but it has the power to attract other events like it (human death) and contribute them to its own perfected experience. In this way, Jesus' death can coconstitute our death. Or to put it another way, we can die *with Jesus*. To the degree we enter into Jesus' death experience or let his experience enter into ours, we die a fuller death, i.e., we open wider our capacity to receive all that God has to give us.

In this sense, the extent of our salvation can be increased by the death of Jesus if we understand salvation as our final relationship with God. The degree of intensity that we could experience in that relationship is always greater when Jesus' experience of that same divine relationship is included in our own. Whether we want to do this or not is our own choice. Whether we recognize the offer, the potential that Jesus' death represents for us depends on our sensitivity to being open to God and God's free activity in our lives. However we perceive it, Jesus' death is always for us. Whether our death is also for Jesus and through him for God is the ultimate question each of us must answer for himself or herself.

Practical Implication

With this understanding of Jesus' death, how would a relational approach respond to the questions raised by the cases seen earlier? The *meaning* of Jesus' death has been spelled out already. From his death we can strengthen our own desire to contribute further to God's experience of us and our capacity to receive from God. This in turn enables God to continue interacting with those still alive by drawing from our experience new possibilities for others.

Regarding the question *why*, Jesus' death illustrates how God is able to bring new possibilities for life out of tragedies when they are experienced in relationship with God. No one was more unjustly killed than Jesus. God's response to this event was not to explain why or to punish the wrongdoers. God's response was to transform that event, give it a creative, new meaning by the possibilities God drew from it. But the new possibilities were (and are) available to those open to feeling them, willing to trust God and experience what God would do with their human capacities stretched to the extreme point. Jesus' death shows us that the greater our capacity to entrust ourselves to God, the more creatively God can transform us toward our fulfillment.

The creative transformation God worked in Jesus is a further indication of what we may expect for ourselves if, like Jesus, we remain open to what God can and will do rather than predetermining what God should do or what we want God to do for us. When we take the latter direction, we limit God. We narrow our capacity to receive and therefore God's capacity to give. Often this means that both we and God are disappointed. But if our primary focus is on God, not ourselves, and if we trust that God will do all that God can do, then *immortality* and *resurrection* are gifts we hope for and enable God to give to us in the fullest possible degree.

In the same way, the field of influence generated by Jesus' death allows us to enter into a deep, internal relationship with God wherein our relative contribution to others, through our contribution to God, is already occurring. The value of this contribution is God's *judgment* of us, or evaluation of how our actual experience furthers God's creative advance. When our contribution is united with and influenced by Jesus' contribution, that judgment is already positive and remains only a question of degree.

The same may be said for our social responsibility. By intensifying every present occasion as fully as possible and staying open to what God can and will do freely with it for the *future*, we contribute to a hopeful future, one that God can effect to the degree our present actions allow. The ultimate shape of the future is not ours to give. Ours is to do what is right in the present, to respond to God's best aim for us here and now. Out of that will come the best possible future.

The present chapter has aimed at explaining Jesus' death in terms of the general relational view put forward in this book. A relational explanation is quite different from a typical theological explanation. Whether the differences are acceptable variations on our common belief or mutually exclusive alternatives is an important question, although it may still be too early to decide. In any event, it will be helpful to summarize the contrasts noted in this book and draw together some final conclusions about when the becoming ceases.

Appendix
When the Becoming Ceases

The approach used in this book is grounded in the more explicit philosophical and theological principles of process thought, primarily as articulated by Alfred North Whitehead. Whitehead's schema, which he preferred to call a philosophy of organism, tries to see each event in its relationship to everything else. This relationship is always dynamic and interdependent. God is no exception. In fact, God is the chief exemplification of what reality is.

A relational theology of death seeks to understand the human experience of death consistently according to the general principles of this metaphysical view. The first part of this Appendix will summarize the interpretations already set forth in the preceding chapters, but will do so in a more systematic and technical way than the individual chapters allowed. Following this presentation, the relational theology of death will be compared with the typical theology of death in order to assess the strengths and limitations of each.

A Relational Theology of Death

The fundamental meaning or value of death is its contribution to God's experience. This is a real contribution to God's experience, an addition or modification of who God actually is. Only a worldview that understands God to be interdependent can make such a claim. If God is understood as independent, as the dominant Western worldview asserts, then death remains ultimately outside God's experience and God's relationship to death is an external one.

In a relational view, the situation is seen differently. Relational thinking does not posit an ontological difference between God and the world. Rather, it assumes an ontological sameness insofar as the primary ontological principle of becoming is verified in all that actually is. Within this metaphysical sameness there is, however, an almost infinite degree of variation, with God being the most complete exemplification of being. In a relational view, God and the world are always necessarily interdependent. They become together. The obvious differences we observe are matters of degree.

Death is the eventual aim of every process of becoming, in the sense that to become some definite configuration of the world is the crowning achievement of every process. In this view, death is interpreted positively as the completion of a process or occasion that began *for the sake of* coming to completion. And because of the dynamic urge toward creativity, every actualized occasion spurs new possibilities that initiate new occasions, sometimes in the same series of development, sometimes in another series.

Death as the completion of discrete occasions of becoming is occurring constantly, a phenomenon Whitehead referred to as "perpetual perishing." Only when death occurs is an event valuable because only then is it fully actual. While in process, occasions are exciting, adventurous, self-creating, but they are also self-contained. No other entity or process of becoming can experience them until they have become what they will be. The final outcome is the fullest satisfaction of every experience of becoming.

The final outcome or satisfaction can then be a real contribution to the whole, to the all-inclusive experience of God's becoming. The discrete events arise out of and contribute back to the whole. For the term of their own becoming, they are radically atomistic, but precisely in this phase of their becoming their experience is isolated. Through perishing, an entity satisfies its urge toward definiteness and becomes valuable for the whole.

Sin affects this sequence as a conditioning factor but not as an originating cause. Because God and the world are necessarily related, sin cannot break that relationship. It can, of course, affect the quality of the relationship. The quality of the becoming can be weakened, lessened, fragmented by sin, and this of course is a significant factor. Because everything is a matter of degrees in a relational view, to lessen the degree of satisfaction and the eventual value of contribution because of sin is most serious. Thus, sin is not negligible in a relational theology of death, but its effect is defined more in terms of the quality of becoming than in the origin of death.

Undoubtedly, the chief motive for our interest in a theology of death is the question of afterlife. The desire to continue our personal, conscious experience beyond death is deep and gripping for most of us. The influence of Greek thinking about the inherent immortality of the soul and the acceptance of Jesus' resurrection as a pledge of personal immortality have combined to make a convincing argument for Christian believers.

Relational thinking is not so decisive about personal immortality. The prospect of continued, subjective experience after perishing requires a special intervention and action by God. This seems to be not inconsistent with relational principles but is not clearly required by them either. Thus, a relational theology does not offer the same assurance as typical theology about personal immortality.

On the other hand, precisely because of its hesitance on this point, relational theology keeps the primacy of God intact. Whether there is personal immortality or not, God receives the life experience of each person as a real contribution to God's becoming. At the same time, if there is personal immortality, God is the indispensable agent of it. Thus, immortality would be viewed not as the inevitable nature of the soul but as a free gift from the gratuity of God.

Drawing upon the resurrection of Jesus and the God whom Jesus revealed, relational theology can advocate a spirit of hope for personal immortality with the accompanying disposition of openness to God who is always primary.

Obviously, if there is no personal immortality, there is no great interest in the resurrection of the dead or the end of the world. These two dominant aspects of early Christian expectation have tended to diminish somewhat in modern times, but they remain important features of Christian belief. Resurrection as a postponed event would appear to be incongruous with an organic philosophy in which processes come into being and perish continuously, but do not begin again once they have perished. Similarly, the end of the world as a ceasing of all becoming and the transition to a permanent, eternal state directly contradicts the ontological principle of relational thinking. If eternity (heaven) is actual, it must become. A nonbecoming state of perfection is impossible in a relational view.

We could, however, speculate about what a relational explanation of these two points might be. Regarding the resurrection, a relational view could see the intimate connection between the body and soul so that what the body becomes for and with the soul, how it enters the soul's experience, is its resurrection. In this view, the resurrection of the body is a continuous process of being prehended by the soul. This process comes to its completion when the soul's becoming ceases—at death. This would mean a continuous and immediate resurrection. If the soul continues in some personal, immortal state after death, the body would share that condition precisely in the manner that it had entered the soul's experiential constitution.

Moreover, if the personal immortality of the soul is effected by God and God alone, then the resurrection of the body in its immortal dimension would also be God's act. In its immediate dimension, the resurrection of the body is the soul's act. In either case, there would be no end-time resurrection in relational thinking similar to the apocalyptic descriptions in Scripture.

This prospect raises at least two important theological questions in addition to the interpretation of biblical passages referring to the end of the world. The first question concerns the final judgment; the other concerns the ultimate correcting of injustices. The two are intimately related. If there is no single, concluding end to the world, there would seem to be no final judgment. And if there is no final judgment, then the hoped-for redress of injustices and vindication of the oppressed also seems to vanish.

Although an absolute end to the world is not really envisioned in relational thought, divine judgment is included as a continuous phase of the becoming process. It consists of God's experience of each completed occasion or entity. How God experiences each occasion is the evaluation of that occasion. The evaluation is framed by two poles: the intrinsic satisfaction relative to the initial possibilities that an entity contributes to God's experience and the relative value of that contribution within the totality of experiences that constitute God's total experience.

The first aspect of judgment is permanent and once-for-all. An entity is what it has become, no more and no less. God cannot change that. The second aspect of judgment is changing and continuous. An entity's value in relation to the whole of becoming creation is ever present (in God) and active. What God can do with one's becoming in relation to the possibilities for future becoming is continuously determined by the ongoing creative advance of the world.

This raises two implications for a relational eschatology and the question of ultimate redress of injustice. The first implication is that any injustice must be redressed within the world process. There is no alternative state of being or becoming where the shortcomings of this world will be remedied. Thus, a strong existential-historical thrust results for a relational eschatology. With this comes a heightened sense of social responsibility and action for justice in the present. The key motive here is the intrinisic correctness of being just. Out of this motive and the experiences that it fosters comes a dominant attitude of hope.

Hope aims at that which cannot be instrumentally produced. It yearns for what goes beyond the achievement of plans and skills. Hope includes these efforts, thus reinforcing the stress on present social commitment, but the ultimate goal of hope lies outside one's own control and power. Thus, a relational understanding of the redress of injustice is not an eventual possession of what one is now denied but a continuous contribution to what others may yet experience.

This position is not likely to have great appeal for those who measure value in terms of their own achievement. Here as elsewhere, relational thinking is holistic, oriented to the total process and its possibilities for new becoming.

All this is borne out in a reflection on Jesus' death. When the faith-claims for Jesus' life and death are interpreted in a relational framework, they express the dipolarity that permeates the whole creative process. In Jesus' life, and preeminently in his death, the contrast between human and divine poles is intensified to the maximum. By becoming this contrast actually, Jesus exemplifies the dipolarity of the world to the fullest degree.

From such an experience, God derives ever new, real possibilities for human becoming and especially for human dying. At the same time, Jesus experiences divine freedom and creative transformation to a unique degree. This dual experience, which constitutes one actual occasion, is everlastingly part of the creative process so that all entities may share its effect by reenacting it in their own experience. The ways this may be done are numerous and so are the corresponding degrees of value to be derived from them.

But the originating event is of cosmic proportions in itself. All occasions within the cosmos participate in it to varying degrees of fullness. In these terms, Jesus' death experience remains unique, universal, and salvific, while his own relationship to God may be understood as such an exemplification of conformal union with God that he is the incarnate Logos of God, the Christ.

Critical Comparison

What real contribution does a relational theology of death make? It can appear to be little more than an apologia for process-relational thinking, especially if all the traditional positions find a place in a relational schema. Then the result is more of a relational translation of typical theology than a relational theology itself.

On the other hand, it can appear that typical theology is being exonerated by showing how historical positions can be made compatible with a contemporary metaphysics that is itself critical of the past.

Neither conclusion would be very satisfying. The former would compromise tradition by making it fit a Procrustean bed of modern making. The latter would compromise relational theology by enervating it of its potential contributions to the tradition. The results of the foregoing exploration instead suggest something more like a dipolar interaction that stimulates both members by intensifying their contrasts.

In this schema, the impact of a typical theology of death on relational thinking appears in at least four areas. First, typical theology pushes the relational understanding of immortality, specifically on the question of personal, subjective experience. For a precisely Christian theology of death, subjective immortality is central. The Easter proclamation about Jesus' resurrection has been taken as a revelation of the destiny intended for each person. Belief in the risen Jesus rather than philosophical arguments about the nature of the soul has nurtured Christian hope and expectation of personal immortality.

It is probably true that this faith assurance has tended to redirect attention away from God's primacy and toward our own felt need or desire to survive after death. The proper priority cannot be restored in an integral Christian theology by eliminating concern for or belief in personal immortality. More is at stake than self-centeredness. The revelation of God in Jesus has uttered a word about immortality that cannot go unheard.

The struggle of relational theology to arrive at a coherent affirmation of this point discloses one of its weaknesses as an appropriate theology for Christian belief. The suggestion put forth in chapter three is a tentative probe into the possibilities of relational thought. The question needs further exploration because it is of decisive importance. The strength of this weakness is, of course, that relational theology forcefully reminds us of the primacy of God and the creatureliness of the rest of us. But if it can go no further, it will be an unsatisfying stance and perhaps an unacceptable one. The main question remains: Can relational theology contribute to traditional belief in subjective immortality or only critique misplaced emphases within that belief? It is an urgent test question that the tradition puts to relational thinking if it is to be an appropriate theology of death.

A second area where the traditional theology stimulates relational thought concerns sin and its connection with death. It is a frequent criticism of process-relational metaphysics (as of other evolutionary-developmental worldviews) that it undervalues the role of evil and suffering. This has a special resonance in Christian theology that has given primary attention to the impact of sin in human history. Of course, the precise connection between sin and death is a matter of ongoing discussion within typical Christian theology. Even so, in a relational view of death, sin would not play the same role as in typical theology. As a result, relational theology can appear to neglect a basic and influential element.

Still, a relational worldview includes the prerequisite notions for a theology of sin. Among these are the divinely offered initial aims; the free, self-creative act of becoming; and the universal interconnectedness of actual entities. From this nucleus a relational theology of sin can be constructed. The concrete and personal effect of sin on individual lives tends, however, to be obscured in a view that is intentionally holistic and organic. The experience of sin can be artificially thinned out when put on the scale of the whole creative process. To the degree that this happens, relational thinking can drift away from the radically personalized encounters of Jesus with sin and evil, and thus lessen its appropriateness as a Christian theology.

Of course, the greatest existential concern about sin and death for most people remains judgment and their ultimate destiny. This bears directly on the question of subjective immortality and the prospect of eternal reward or punishment. Here again, relational theology's initial position can seem to mitigate all this, not only because of its ambivalence regarding subjective immortality but also because of its view of inclusive divine judgment. A fuller explanation of the degrees of satisfaction and evaluation that relational thought envisions would, however, convey the same message about the ultimate importance of personal decisions and their impact on the future. How effectively this is done as an appeal to do good and avoid evil is a major communications task that faces not just relational theology but all Christian theology.

A third area where typical theology challenges a relational theology of death is the interpretation of Jesus' death. This event coupled, of course, with the resurrection is at the center of Christian belief about death and immortality. Any theology that attempts to give appropriate expression to this belief must convey what Jesus' death has meant. If Jesus' death is the decisive occurrence that spells the difference between fulfillment and frustration, between love and loss, between union and isolation, then a relational theology of death should be able to explain how this is so.

Relational Christology up to now has not looked closely at this issue. Attention has been directed more toward the identity of Jesus as God's revelation and transforming agent. The precise significance of his death and its effect on the history of humankind has not been addressed extensively.

As suggested in chapter seven, the groundwork for an appropriate presentation of Jesus' death is already laid in the relational principles of universal interconnectedness, prehension and reenactment, and the overriding goal of creative advance through intensive experiences. How all this may be assembled and related to the traditional claims for Jesus is a task yet to be done thoroughly.

There is an inherent tension in relational thinking with any claim that would go beyond the fundamental principles governing its worldview. This is seen most clearly in the understanding of God and God's relation to the world, but the same problematic arises regarding Jesus. Of course, there is an intrinsic tension in Christology to begin with, stemming from the claim that in Jesus full humanity and full divinity are united. Relational theology offers a way of interpreting the experience and union of these two poles that is consistent with its own fundamental dipolar view of reality. Whether it is equally consistent with Christian belief remains to be seen conclusively.

Nonetheless, the death of Jesus holds the same preeminent place in a relational Christology as in typical Christology. The ultimate importance of finalizing any process of becoming is directly applicable to Jesus' death. Only when finalized can his process of becoming have real value for others, including God. Thus, relational theology would clearly affirm that Jesus "had to die" to be the Christ. Beyond this, the fuller grasp of what his death entails and how it is to be interpreted and reenacted is as elusive to relational theology as it is to typical theology.

There is one other aspect of typical theologies of death that merits a brief mention as a fourth area of examination for relational theology. This is the interaction between the living and the dead. In Christian history this has been generally referred to as the communion of saints, and a far-reaching piety has been cultivated on the basis of a real linkage between those on earth (the church militant), those in the interim state (the church suffering), and those in heaven (the church triumphant).

Relational theology addresses this with its organic emphasis and general principle of the interrelatedness of all things. Relational thinking describes in a general way how this interaction occurs, but by and large it has not developed this insight concretely enough. Here the symbols, rites, devotions of people can prod relational thinkers to explore their own views in a more usable way. In general, the Christian feeling for the solidarity of believers and the expressions of this in prayer and devotion can stimulate relational theology to maximize the social-organic character of its reflection, and thus present death as less of an atomistic event and more as an occasion in a society of events that share a real union through internal relations.

Relational theology has its own contributions to make to the tradition. Perhaps the most important of these is not strictly theological. Relational theology is developed from an explicit metaphysical, philosophical system. It offers a programmatic alternative to typical theology because the particular philosophical system underlying relational theology is quite distinct from the philosophical systems previously employed by Christian theology. The general benefit from this is that typical theology can be examined in a thoroughgoing, tough-minded way that can open up new directions, new insights, and new challenges.

The major question, however, is the acceptability of the relational metaphysic. Clearly, its validity is not self-evident and has in fact generated widespread and increasing debate. Nonetheless, its respectability as an important contemporary philosophical system seems established even as weaknesses and ambiguities continue to be explored. A relational theologian needs to keep one eye on the continuing philosophical discussion even while working out the implications for theological issues. This leads to the prospect of a genuinely constructive and speculative theology.

Such a theology can dialogue creatively with typical theology in order to formulate a more coherent, adequate articulation of Christian belief. For example, the uneven joining of Jewish apocalyptic and Greek philosophical elements in a typical theology of death can perhaps be seen more clearly when typical theology is rethought in terms that are neither apocalyptic nor simply Greek-philosophical. More than that, relational thought can provide an alternative framework for interpreting and expressing more coherently the originating beliefs, especially regarding the interim state, the resurrection of the dead, and particular/general judgment.

A second major contribution of relational theology to typical theology is the unequivocal primacy given to God. There is no dichotomy in relational theology; God and world are always interdependent. The task is to respect the limits on our desires and self-importance so that God remains primary.

At the same time, God's primacy is described in terms of becoming. This is translated in terms of feeling, taking in, making one's own. The God of relational theology is very active, very intimate, and very feeling. Whereas the human, personal focus appears to be sacrificed in a relational emphasis, especially regarding subjective immortality, it is really located more appropriately in a relational view. The locus of the fullest feeling and life experience is not in what one can hold on to forever for oneself but in what one can give away to God everlastingly.

To arrive genuinely at such a position requires profound awareness of oneself as a creature, as less than God but valuable to God. Relational theology challenges typical theology to face this issue directly, to reexamine its motives and arguments for subjective immortality, and to insure that God is primary.

Relational thought counterbalances its caution and even resistance to overstressing subjective immortality with a strong emphasis on the present as having preeminent value. The present is when becoming occurs; it is the creative moment and in a strict sense the only actual moment. What becomes now has everything to do with what the future will become. It conditions the very possibilities for becoming that God can offer.

At the same time, the present is not seen in isolation from the past and the future. There is a continuous flow from the past into the present toward the future. But the possibilities and therefore the real potential for the future are determined in the present. This view has direct bearing on the typical notion of God foreseeing from all eternity everything that will occur and having a plan for the course of human history.

Relational theology forces a revision of the typical idea of providence and its shadow side, theodicy. The question for relational theology is not so much why does God allow evil and suffering to occur but where is God luring us in response to evil experiences once they occur. Such a view in turn can impel believers to a more intense and open encounter with the living God who shares intimately every present moment and seeks to share with us the next best possibility. God is no less providential in relational theology, but divine providence is exercised in a radically different way.

Finally, and extending this emphasis to the present, relational thought encourages a working through of the typical view of eschatology. The exact sense in which the end of the world is to be understood is not perfectly clear in the tradition. Indeed, belief in subjective immortality carries along with it some sense of continued being and living, and to that degree becoming. Relational theology underscores this line of thought and carries it further, suggesting a different image of the end of the world, or perhaps even the image of no end at all. In the latter case, any number of implications appear, not least of which is the problem of injustice and the suffering of the innocent. Whether removing the prospect of an end time and final judgment will increase existential commitment to justice or further weaken the energy of that commitment is hard to say. At least, relational theology forces a reexamination of the nature of the end and from that perspective our responsibility for the present.

This work was conceived as both a pastoral and theological reflection. There is a great gap between the immediate, concrete experiences in which questions about death arise and the abstract, philosophical reflection in which relational theology is couched. How much that gap has been narrowed in this book is for each reader to decide. For myself, the project continues until the becoming ceases.